A celebration of irish guide dogs
for the blind

Independence

Written by
Caroline O'Doherty

Photography
Robert Doyle
and Marc O'Sullivan,
OSD Photo Agency

First published 2006

ISBN 10:   1-85635-540-3
ISBN 13:   978-1-85635-540-7

Published by Irish Guide Dogs for the Blind
Written by Caroline O'Doherty
Photography by Robert Doyle and Marc O'Sullivan OSD Photography
Design and layout by Edward Butt
Printed by Colour Books

Trade Enquiries Columbia Mercier Distribution
55a Spruce Avenue,
Stillorgan Park Ind. Estate,
Blackrock, Co. Dublin

INTRODUCTION

IRISH Guide Dogs for the Blind was co-founded in 1976 by the late Mrs Mary Dunlop and our current President Mr Jim Dennehy. At that time there was no opportunity for training with a guide dog for blind and vision-impaired people living in Ireland other than travelling to Britain. For many people, this was not possible.

The success of the organisation to date is a testimony to the vision and commitment of the founders and those who worked alongside them during those early days – many of these people are featured in this book.

From humble beginnings, Irish Guide Dogs for the Blind has grown to take its place amongst the finest guide dog schools in the world with a reputation built on innovation and quality of service to clients.

Our services now extend to the provision of guide dogs, orientation and mobility training (long cane), independent living skills training, and a child mobility programme which is operated in conjunction with the Department of Education and Science.

Recently, we have introduced the assistance dogs programme, which provides fully-trained dogs to families of children with autism. The impact of this service on the families has been profoundly positive and, along with building the capacity of this programme, our focus is on extending the service to benefit other people with disabilities such as deafness and those whose disabilities are not related to vision or hearing.

From our headquarters in Cork we provide training and support to a growing national client base. We employ over 50 staff and rely on – literally – thousands of volunteers, who work in every aspect of the organisation from the training of dogs to fundraising and administration. Volunteers have been at the heart of the organisation from the beginning and are rightly cherished for their commitment and practical support.

From the beginning, the organisation was based on the principle of making our services available to all: we do not charge for training or for the lifetime of support provided to clients.

Self-reliance has been a guiding principle of the organisation. We came through some very difficult days where the organisation survived only through the extraordinary commitment of the board, staff, volunteers, and the overwhelming generosity of the public.

Over 80 percent of our operating budget is derived from fundraising and donations. Our nationwide network of over 100 branches is at the heart of our success in this area. The public continues to generously support Irish Guide Dogs for the Blind, thanks to the branches and supporters who create the opportunity to donate - whether in the street with a collecting bucket or through an event or activity, they make it happen year after year.

For some time, our objective has been to increase the amount of government funding for our work. We are very grateful for the current level of day-to-day support as well as the money received for capital projects but we continue to strive for a greater recognition of the importance of our work with a more meaningful level of government funding.

Our plans focus strongly on developing training capacity and enhancing our services. We aim to ensure that services are delivered in a timely, client-centred manner which will ultimately lead to the development of other training facilities in Dublin and, in time, in regional centres.

We are planning for significant growth in the number of people trained and increasing our supports in education and awareness to make sure society continues to facilitate full participation by blind and vision-impaired people as well as people with other disabilities.

We are conscious of our role in developing an awareness of the importance of eye care and will continue to work to ensure a greater level of understanding among the public and support from government.

Through our work, lives are changed for the better, individuals benefit, and society benefits; our future development will ensure that participation is not just an aspiration, but also a reality for those that we are privileged to serve.

Charles Daly, Chairman of the board of directors

ACKNOWLEDGEMENTS

Heartfelt thanks go to the following for their assistance in the creation of this book:

Andrew Downes

Mary Frances Fahy

Mary Feehan

Frances Jones

Gerry Kelly

Brian Lougheed, Digipix

Lisa McCormack

Anna McHugh

Anne Marie O'Brien & Mark Hanratty

Pat & Cara O'Doherty

Joanne O'Doherty, Mario Wallemann & Nathan O'Doherty-Wallemann

An Post

Eoin Quinn

Liam Sweeney

Tim Vaughan

Patrons

Irish Guide Dogs for the Blind

Cllr. Michael Ahern,
Lord Mayor of Cork

Cllr. Niall O'Brolachain,
Mayor of Galway City

Cllr. Vincent Jackson,
Lord Mayor of Dublin

AN POST
Sponsor

TO say something would fit on a postage stamp normally means it is small and insignificant but in the world of philately nothing could be further from the truth.

Every stamp tells a story, whether it is about a person of influence or a place of interest, a natural wonder or man-made landmark, a single striking happening or an evolution of events over time.

In the summer of 2006 it was the turn of Irish Guide Dogs for the Blind to make its mark on the catalogue of Irish stamps: an occasion that was to prove as historic for An Post as it was for Irish Guide Dogs.

An Post receives about 500 requests and suggestions for new stamps every year but only around 40 can be granted, so just securing a place in the production programme is a feat.

In addition, the very fact that Irish Guide Dogs for the Blind was celebrating its 30th anniversary posed a challenge to protocol, as Barney Whelan, head of business development and corporate affairs at An Post, explains. "We would normally have 25, 50, 75 or 100 years on anniversary stamps but we made an exception in this case."

And that was not just the decision of An Post, as every new stamp has to be approved by the Government. The process may sound bureaucratic but it underlines the importance the State attaches to Irish stamps.

"A stamp only has to bear the name of the country and the price because, essentially, it is just a receipt for a service. But stamps have come to represent so much more than that, and we're always thinking about how we can optimise the design of our stamps so that we have something that portrays the country in a wide variety of ways."

Once the 30th anniversary stamp was approved in principle, the design committee got to work on ideas for how it should look. That was the tricky part.

"My idea was that we had to see if we could illustrate what I called the 'moment of enablement' because, if you are trying to illustrate the impact that a guide dog has on a person's life, you have to show that it has enabled that person to be mobile and to participate in life in a way they would not be able to without the dog.

"My fellow members of the design advisory team said: 'Fine, Barney, but how do we illustrate a "moment of enablement"?' I have to admit I wasn't too sure!"

Putting the concept into visual form did prove a challenge but eventually a picture emerged of a dog stepping forward, the hand of its owner safely holding the harness while preparing to take that first step too.

The design team was keen to use a variety of colours and include street furniture or a pedestrian crossing to place the dog and owner in a particular environment but a consultation with experts in visual impairment quickly changed their minds.

"They came back to us with a set of guidelines that had four key elements: font, meaning the type of lettering; colour contrast; shades; and shapes. A visually impaired person who still has some sight can see things if you present them in the correct way so we had to start thinking about how the stamp did its job for these customers."

The finished product, with artwork by illustrator Steve Simpson, was a simple but strong image in two starkly contrasting deep but vibrant colours, with the lettering and numbers in a large, clear font, and the price replicated in Braille.

One third of a million were printed, some going into general circulation and others bought by stamp collectors all over the world. The response was excellent and An Post was pleased both for the design team and its subject.

"Guide Dogs is an organisation that has two main levels of activity: it provides a service for blind people and it fundraises. The stamp commemorated the service, but a key element of fundraising in the charity sector is raising awareness and I think the stamp helped in that area too. We'd like to think it did two jobs in one."

Left to right: Professor Iseult McCarthy, *Chairperson of the Stamp Design Advisory Committee*; Mr Barney Whelan, *Head of Corporate Affairs and Business Development, An Post* and Mr Steve Simpson, *Stamp Designer*.

TOM & GILLIAN APLIN
Vice-chairman and fundraiser

THE chairman of any organisation has to be innovator, leader and arbitrator all in one. As Tom Aplin prepares to take over the chairmanship of Irish Guide Dogs for the Blind, he can be confident he already has that last trait in the bag.

Tom is a rugby referee and if the prospect of 30 fired-up rugby players staring down at him doesn't faze him, not even the most spirited discussion around the boardroom table will.

Rugby is just one of Tom's passions. Originally in sales and marketing, he and his wife, Gillian, a former Aer Lingus stewardess, found their lives taking an unexpected turn after they lost their daughter, Sally, to cancer when she was only in her early thirties.

"Sally lived and breathed animals," Gillian says. "We had dogs, guinea pigs and 26 rabbits at one stage because of Sally! We were on a family holiday in Wexford once when she was little and she wanted to go pony trekking and that was it – she was totally hooked."

Sally went to university when she finished school but all the time she was itching to be outdoors working with animals. Eventually she got her wish when she rented stables at Kilternan in the foothills of the Dublin Mountains and set up her own livery service.

Her enthusiasm was infectious and soon Tom and Gillian were learning to ride too. Even Sally's brother, Mark, an investment banker in England, became smitten and keeps his own horse in the countryside for weekend escapes.

When Sally died, her heartbroken parents looked at all she had created and decided they didn't want it to die with her. They made a major change in their lives, taking over the running of the stables, and through the daily sights and sounds of clip-clopping hooves, tossing manes, muddy wellingtons, laughing children and reassuring words, Sally's dream lives on.

For many years, Tom and Gillian have been near neighbours and friends of Peg Lyons, one of the country's first guide dog owners, and they have long been active members of the Dun Laoghaire-Rathdown Branch of Irish Guide Dogs for the Blind.

The branch's fundraising summer fair, theatre nights and choral performances have become essential features of the area's social calendar and Tom has completed a sponsored cycle around Cuba for the organisation.

He and Gillian also manage to combine two interests in one by doing the rounds of horse and pony events, setting up information and merchandise stalls.

"Fundraising has become very competitive and people have to be quite innovative; but, as a charity, we are unique in that we can show the final product to people who donate. No matter how charming we are – it's the dogs that win people over," says Tom.

So how innovative does Tom plan to be as a chairman? "I have lots of ideas. I'd love to see us extend the breeding programme further and produce dogs for countries, such as in Eastern Europe, where there is no tradition of guide dog training.

"And I'd love to see us expand the assistance dogs programme for autistic children. That has really shown us where creative thinking can take us. We also have to continue to build up our puppy-walking in Dublin and Leinster because we have to remember that, while there's a natural affiliation with the organisation in Munster, and Cork in particular, half our clients are from the east coast.

"At the same time, our branch network is the cornerstone of our strength and we have to continue to improve and develop that. The people standing outside shopping centres with collection boxes not only raise money but also awareness, and awareness is so important in today's society. Kids today are lovely but they can be insular – society is driving them that way. Everyone's so busy and it's easy to spoil kids and make them too focused on themselves.

"We need them to think outside of themselves if they are going to be our supporters in the future. In fact, we all need to think outside our own box and be prepared to take chances and make changes – because, if you don't, the box just closes in on you."

JOE BARRETT
Former chairman

FARMING when Joe Barrett was a boy was all muck and muscle with very little assistance from machines.

Joe pondered the family tradition briefly - and went swiftly into chartered accountancy. It seemed an easier choice until Irish Guide Dogs for the Blind got its paws on him.

His involvement began with a phone call from one of the founder members, fellow Corkman, Jim Dennehy, who explained his idea for the organisation and asked for advice on how to set it up. Joe was happy to oblige and talked Jim and co-founder Mary Dunlop through the financial legalities.

"I thought that was the end of it, but a month or two later they told me they had formed a company and needed signatories to the articles of incorporation. Suddenly I was a director."

He may have escaped the toil of the farm, but there was no way Joe was going to avoid getting his hands dirty on this assignment.

"I hated fundraising," he confesses. "I remember my first time out. I got evening Masses to do and it was New Year's Eve and snowing. I felt very sorry for myself."

The efforts of every fundraiser who stood in the cold on a winter's night paid off, however, and within a few years the organisation had enough in the bank to buy the old farmhouse and land in Cork that today is its headquarters and training centre.

Money was always tight and when board meetings and other appointments necessitated travel around the country, economies were achieved by piling everyone into the back of a bright orange Volkswagen minibus.

The appearance was more hippy rock band than board of directors, but it did the trick. Joe remembers one occasion on which he and Jim Dennehy splashed out on the train fare to Dublin in a snowstorm because they considered it too perilous to drive but Mary Dunlop could not be dissuaded.

"'Don't be ridiculous,' she told me. 'I have driven in much worse conditions in Egypt during the war.' She had driven an ambulance in North Africa during World War II. She must have thought we were terrible wimps."

Joe was chairman from 1981 until 1996 when he resigned to let in new blood. During that time, he witnessed great change, not just in the services provided, but in society's attitude to blindess too.

"One man who came to the centre in the early days didn't know how to tie his shoe laces because his mother had always done it for him. I believe we helped change lives. That was payback enough for me – even if it did mean I ended up on a farm after all!"

SALLY BAXTER & JACINTA BREEN
Volunteers

SALLY Baxter and Jacinta Breen are neighbours, friends and co-conspirators.

They moved to Ovens in Co Cork a year apart; their children are the same ages and in the same classes at school; they both love dogs and tennis, and they like nothing better than to share cups of coffee and long chats.

It was only to be expected that when one of them spotted an advertisement seeking volunteers to help out at the headquarters of the Irish Guide Dogs for the Blind that the other would be reading over her shoulder.

Now every Wednesday, and other days as required, the pair head off to the National Headquarters and Training Centre and report for whatever duty needs attending to.

Sally has filled in at reception and loves anything to do with phones and computers. Jacinta gets stuck into accounts, paperwork and odd jobs - anything but phones and computers.

"One of these days I'll get her on to the computers," Sally vows. "No you won't!" says Jacinta. "It's a fear I have that I'd delete everything. I'm afraid to touch a button."

Sally and Jacinta are relative newcomers to the volunteer army and it was with trepidation that they turned up the first day. "I didn't like to ask in advance what we'd be doing. I thought we might be cleaning out dog pooh and I didn't know what to wear!"

They haven't yet been assigned to kennel duties but they're willing. "I'm delighted," says Sally. "I know I'm doing work for Guide Dogs but actually Guide Dogs is doing a lot for me. I left work when my second child was born and that was 13 years ago.

"A lot has changed in the workplace and this is getting me back to the modern day. It's good for the kids to see 'look, mammy is able to do other things'."

Jacinta, a former hairdresser, has also been busy working in the home and, despite her computer phobia, is pleased to be back in the workplace. "Even though I enjoy it, I know it's serious business and it gives you a sense of pride to know you hold a responsibility towards the organisation.

"People say to me: 'That's something I would love to do as well but I wouldn't know how to go about it.' Well, I wouldn't have known about it either only Sally spotted the ad.

"I got her into tennis and she got me into Guide Dogs. I'm not sure what we'll get into next but we'll think of something."

Pictured left tot right
Mark Breen, Jacinta Breen,
Sally Baxter, Kayleigh Baxter

JOE BOLLARD
Guide dog owner

TALK to Joe. Joe will know. Joe's been there. People automatically think of Joe Bollard when there's a query or concern around blindness or disability in general.

But while he loves to lend a listening ear or helpful hand, Joe sounds a word of warning: he doesn't know everything. Not even after seven decades of blindness, five guide dogs, one autobiography, numerous careers, and countless travels.

"I'm still learning," he says. "I only know you can't shock me and you can't embarrass me. I've been around the world twice and I'm a musician, so I've mixed with the best … and the worst."

Joe was one of a family of 13 children born in inner city Dublin in the 1930s and he was blinded at two years of age by a medical mishap to this day not fully explained. He had a rough-and-tumble childhood marked by poverty and upheaval but also by the discovery of music.

Song and the piano became the tools he used to express and support himself and later his growing family. They took him through the showband era, on to cabaret, and into his current role as singer and organist at Masses, weddings, and funerals.

He also creates backing tracks in his kitchen-cum-studio for other musicians and he is editor and reporter for 'Focus' magazine, the monthly audio publication of the National Council for the Blind of Ireland.

"There aren't enough hours in the day," he says, and that's despite rising every morning without fail at 6.30am. After a brisk walk with his guide dog Dillon along Bray promenade, Joe logs on to his computer and begins dealing with the emails that flood into him from all around the world.

"I get contacted from Africa, Asia, America – it's fascinating to hear how blind people live around the world. I've had articles sent to me from Nigeria and Senegal and I think how I can run upstairs and switch on the computer to communicate, while for others mobility training means trying to find their way around with a branch of tree used as a cane."

Much of Joe's travels have been with the Blazing Saddles fundraising cycle group with whom he has wheeled his way around the world on tandem since 1991. "My big retirement trip was a cycle across America in 2003," he says, adding with a whisper: "But rumour has it I might be making a comeback in 2007."

He says his ever-patient wife, Sarah, will just sigh and shake her head knowingly but he doesn't know how he'll explain his absence to devoted Dillon. "We're not supposed to compare the dogs, but Dillon really is the cleverest I have had. He was here before. He was some human who has been reincarnated as a dog.

"They say for a blind person the dog is our eyes but they're more than that. They're an extension of our personality. People look at Joe Bollard and say he is mad and extrovert and so is his dog. But I can't be mad all the time and you must keep your dog under control too. He's a dog, not a machine, and he'll do doggy things if I don't remind him not to."

Joe believes in constant refresher training and has no qualms about making Dillon retrace his steps and approach an obstacle again if he doesn't get it just right first time. "A dog taught something at 12 months old isn't going to remember it for life unless he's reminded."

He has a natural empathy with guide dogs on this point. Joe is a recovering alcoholic – a legacy of the heady showband days – and, though he hasn't touched a drop in years, he would never be so presumptuous as to think he couldn't put a foot wrong again.

Joe recounted his personal battles in his 1997 autobiography, 'Out of Sight', which he says was written partly out of his natural extroversion and partly out a desire to help others.

"It was to say: I'm me, I'm Joe, a person whose eyes don't work, a person who has coped with alcoholism and a person who knows that, even when you're blind, there's a light at the end of the tunnel."

VICTOR BOYHAN
Branch member and former board member

IN the orphanage where Victor Boyhan grew up, the blind seamstress was a great source of friendship and fascination as she battled good-humouredly to repair the wear and tear 160 boys inflicted on their uniforms.

She had a German shepherd to guide her – much to the envy of Victor and his pal, Paul McGrath, who admired the gentle animal. "She used to tell us the dog was great company and I tend to equate a guide dog with companionship as much as mobility," Victor says.

The boys grew up and left the orphanage – Paul becoming a public figure as successful international footballer and Victor becoming a public representative as member of his local Dun Laoghaire-Rathdown County Council; but those early memories came back to him years later when he spotted a newspaper notice about a new branch of Irish Guide Dogs for the Blind.

Victor was already involved in fundraising for his political party, the Progressive Democrats, and he readily began devising money-spinners for Irish Guide Dogs too.
He also became deeply interested in policy formulation and served for a period on the board of the organisation during which he loved throwing out ideas for discussion.

"In Guide Dogs we focus a lot on the dog but you can not survive with a dog alone. There is the physical, emotional and social side of being visually impaired. I think services in Ireland can be fragmented; but people aren't fragmented. You have desire to be mobile, ambitious, glamorous, successful, in love and in relationships – all in the one person.

"Providing a guide dog is hugely important because it gives independence, mobility and dignity but that's only the beginning, not the full story. If the dog gets you out into the community, we should be working to ensure that once you get there, there are jobs and social networks and whatever other services and supports are needed. My own ambition for Guide Dogs is that we would have the resources to do that."

Victor's personal ambitions include a return to the county council in the next local elections but in the meantime he serves on the national executive of the Progressive Democrats. Unusually for a political party activist, he would definitely not promise to flood Irish Guide Dogs for the Blind with funds if his political career took him to the top.

"What makes the organisation unique is its voluntary nature because that gives the public a role, and when people get involved in organisations, that's what really makes a community.

"People might say all our problems would be solved if we were bankrolled by the State but we would lose the input of the public and that's irreplaceable."

Victor and Juno.

ANGELA BRADLEY
Fundraiser

IN the Isle of Man, where Angela Bradley was born, she saw another side to the picture postcard image of the quaint horse-drawn trams that drew tourists in their droves to the Douglas promenade.

When the animals were worn out from work, they were often herded on to ships and sent off for slaughter. Angela was only a child, but her mother's outrage at the practice taught her an unforgettable lesson about fighting for a good cause.

"I was brought up to love collecting. My mother always had us doing something. It began with the Red Cross and we sold posies of white heather for the Lifeboats too. But then my mother founded a home for old horses and that took over."

The Isle of Man Home of Rest for Old Horses at Bulrhenny, which today is run as a charitable trust and is home to over 60 retired horses, ponies and donkeys, began when Angela's feisty mother boarded a boat to check on the condition of horses for export and refused to get off without them.

"She famously brandished a whip at the crew. It was like a crusade. Now this is a crusade with me."

Angela's crusade is collecting for Irish Guide Dogs for the Blind. She came to Ireland to study at university and, since retiring after 40 years teaching at Rathgar Junior School in south Dublin, has devoted herself full-time to voluntary fundraising.

"My husband, Anton, was in hospital for five and a half years before he died and I was terribly lonely. I took a lot of time thinking what I would do and then I thought, why not go back to those happy days as a child when I was out collecting?"

Angela is thankful she has never needed to brandish a whip, just a smile. "You meet such nice people and it brings out the best in you and in them.

"My mother didn't have money to look after horses but my dad was a monumental sculptor and a client of his left a legacy that bought 40 acres of land and a farmhouse and cottage. My mother always said Bulrhenny was built on faith, that if you have faith, things will work out.

"Guide Dogs has deepened my faith. I believe it to be a very special charity because it involves the interaction of people and animals. Animals are also a part of God's wonderful creation and I am so sure he intended that humans should be the stewards, not exploiters, of them. My mother knew that instinctively. I'm glad she passed it on to me."

Angela Bradley
and Floss.

TERESA BRANDON
Branch member

KILKENNY'S famed fortress walls have withstood all sorts since medieval times but they offer no defence against the irresistible appeal of the city's canine citizens.

Once a year, the historic streets prepare for a welcome invasion and give way to the Irish Guide Dogs for the Blind sponsored dog walk.

The jolly spectacle begins at Kilkenny Castle, once the seat of Strongbow, King of Leinster, and the cavalcade of dogs and owners moves off in regal style, led by a pipe band as it descends on the city centre. Then the real fun begins – the fancy dress show.

Among those leading the charge each year is Teresa Brandon of the Kilkenny branch of Irish Guide Dogs for the Blind who never fails to be moved by the way the community opens its heart for the occasion.

"Members of the committee visit the local schools and talk to the fifth and six classes about the Guide Dog Centre and its wonderful work with the blind. It's incredible they way they respond. They take the sponsorship cards and collect the money and then turn up on the day having made a fantastic effort with their pets."

"We have dogs in Kilkenny jerseys, dogs in socks, dogs in prams – it's a great bit of fun. We hold a raffle afterwards and prize-giving which adds extra excitement, but really it's not competitive – it's just a great day out."

Teresa joined Irish Guide Dogs for the Blind in 1998 on the urging of her daughter who was already a member. "Donna was working on reception in the hotel where the branch held their meetings and she got to know the members so that's how she started. My mother died in 1998 and I was feeling a bit sad. I thought it might help to get involved in something and Donna encouraged me to join."

"Mother was without her sight for the last five years of her life but she was a very strong, energetic person and was always positive. I thought joining Guide Dogs would be a positive way of doing something in her memory."

The dog walk is just one event in the branch's annual fundraising calendar but Teresa, who works part-time at the local Aut Even Hospital, finds people are always generous with their time and donations.

She heaps similar praise on her fellow committee members too, and pays special tribute to the late Ann Phelan, a dynamic and dedicated member who passed away in 2005 and is sadly missed.

"You could not do this without the help of people like Ann and all our friends who never fail to turn out in all weather. We ask a lot of them but once they know it's for Guide Dogs, they're behind us."

Robbie Brandon, Teresa & Reay Brandon, Daughter Donna Millett and Donna's Dog Kiara. Photo by Anthony Dawson.

PEGGY BRAY
Fundraiser and former board member

PEGGY Bray always knew how to turn heads.

If it wasn't her broad American accent that attracted attention as she toured pubs with her collection boxes, it was the flamboyant straw hat she wore festooned with ribbons, bows and toy dogs.

Then there were her cars. Often her Morris 1100 was barely visible under the giant papier mache guide dog she made to sit on the roof. Her daughter Lynn jokes she was only sorry it wasn't big enough to hide the "three mortified children" who were brought along on their mother's colourful fundraising ventures.

Then Peggy shipped over from the United States her late mother's car – a 1966 Ford Mustang. Long, sleek and left-hand-driven, the exotic automobile with the sprightly pensioner at the wheel was quite a sight meandering up and down the narrow roads of her adopted home in Passage West, Cork.

"They called me Mustang Peg," she says, casting a fond eye over the faithful motor still sitting in her yard. "Mustang Peg will ride again!" she promises.

Peggy got involved in Irish Guide Dogs for the Blind through the antics of Frisco, a free-spirited golden retriever named after San Francisco, the city that was her United States home.

Frisco liked to wander and Peggy had to do all the retrieving. She thought obedience training might help and signed up for the classes run by the organisation's co-founder, Mary Dunlop, who used the subscriptions to raise funds for guide dog training.

Frisco never did learn manners but his owner acquired a whole new interest and while her husband Charlie was at sea captaining ships for oil companies, Peggy began charting her own course through the early days of the Guide Dogs.

"I don't know anything about dogs. Oh, I think they're marvellous and I know a lot about loving them, but not about training them. That's a mystery to me. But I do know people. I say to people, I'm not asking you for everything you got. If everybody just gave a buck we'll be okay. Then people don't feel obliged – but they still give."

Peggy survived childhood polio and, in recent years, a stroke and cancer, but she has never let a little illness get her down. Even tales of her mishaps are related with mirth.

When well into her sixties, she canoed down the Lee to raise funds only to be swept into the path of an overhanging branch. Her glasses were yanked off her nose and she was forced into a capsize, from which she emerged squinting and soaking to wave triumphantly to the alarmed onlookers on the banks.

As ever, every head was turned in her direction.

Peggy and Jack Russell Baby with a photograph of her wedding day.

SEAMUS & MARIAN BRENNAN
Fundraisers

SEAMUS and Marian Brennan make a rare admission for people involved with Irish Guide Dogs for the Blind.

"We're cat people," says Marian, nodding to their rotund tabby Tiger lounging in the sun outside their home at Knockcroghery, Co Roscommon. As well as sun-bathing, Tiger enjoys bicycle rides, tummy rubs and chasing rabbits and her owners wouldn't dream of disturbing her charmed existence by introducing a canine companion.

Besides, few dogs could keep up with the Brennans when they go walkies.

Seamus averages six fundraising marathons a year, speed-walking his way through the streets of cities like Dublin, Belfast, London, Edinburgh and New York, and passing out the panting runners as he goes.

Between events and daily exercise, he covers well in excess of 2,000 miles on foot each year. But there was a time he wouldn't walk 200 yards.

"He wasn't a walker at all," laughs Marian. "I didn't drive when the children were small so I would walk everywhere pushing a pram and it took nothing out of me but Seamus wouldn't walk up the road."

Now, while her late-convert husband takes on the big mileage, Marian contents herself with mini-marathons and half-marathons.

"Sure they're only warm-ups," Seamus teases her. He has been teased himself - he did the women's mini-marathon one year with Marian's Irish Countrywomen's Association group, dressed up as a woman and running the gauntlet of wolf whistles all along Dublin's O'Connell Street. "He loved it really," Marian says.

The pair became involved with Irish Guide Dogs for the Blind after hearing an advertisement for a sponsored walk. They already fundraised for heart charities and organisations for the mentally handicapped and instantly decided it would take nothing out of them to clock up a few more miles for another good cause.

Seamus's army background means he was well accustomed to exercise but since he retired, he maintains there is nothing like his daughter's house renovation project for keeping fit. "All that up and down ladders. Walking is nothing after that."

He and Marian are also mad about dancing and love weekends away waltzing and jiving to the hits of the sixties while Marian further boosts her exercise regime with bouts of running around after frantic brides-to-be.

She is a floral arranger for weddings and grows a lot of the flowers in her own back garden where the only plant she doesn't have time for is laurel.

"We don't deserve laurels for what we do. Walking and fundraising is a doddle when you see what some people have to cope with in life. We're as spoilt as the cat really."

TESSIE BUCKLEY
Fundraiser

NOT many dogs can boast of getting a Garda escort for walkies but then walkies in Cloughduv is not your average dog walk.

Tessie Buckley organises the mass gathering of dogs and owners the first Sunday in July each year when the narrow, winding roads around the Co Cork village become one long twisting snake of wagging tails and clattering feet.

"There's a great bit of craic. There is every breed and every size – of dog and people!"

Tessie organised the first walk to raise funds for a sick child 15 years ago. It was such a success that, even though the child recovered, locals urged her to run it again. She did it for Irish Guide Dogs for the Blind and has made it an annual event ever since.

It was her love of animals – she has four corgis and 10 cats - and her family's first-hand experience of blindness that made her think of the organisation.

When she was a child, her father lost an eye in a car accident. He worked in a quarry and, with a wife and four children to support, he was lucky to keep his job. "To lose one eye was hard enough. We often thought what must it be like to lose both."

She found out a few years ago when she contracted a virus and lost her sight temporarily. "It was some fright to get. I thought I would be looking for a guide dog myself. Since then we've put more effort in."

"The fundraising is hard work but I say to people who dither about helping, you might need a dog yourself one day. I know that for a fact now."

Tessie's passion for the organisation is known across the water in England where her late brother, Danny Mullane, fundraised without fail every year through the Irish Centre in Woolwich.

She has great support locally too where she has several committed helpers. "We bum donations and we bum prizes. We are great bums! We'll knock on every door and we'll ask everyone. Where one fails, another tries. I'd ask the Pope for money."

On walk day, local gardai do traffic duty, her husband John Joe drives ahead with loudspeakers playing records, and a minibus trails behind to pick up people suffering from exertion or heat.

It doesn't get many passengers. The Cornerstone Bar in Crookstown donates cold drinks and sandwiches for the finishers but Tessie holds the tickets that vouch for their participation.

"I stand half way along the route so no-one gets their picnic if they turn back before that," she says. "And sure, once they come half way, they always finish."

GORDON BURROWS
Branch chairman and former board member

MAKING a success of a venture isn't always rocket science – and Gordon Burrows should know.

As an engineer with the National Board for Science and Technology in the 1970s, he was instrumental in getting the Irish space programme off the ground. Officials at the time were doubtful that any good would come of Ireland joining the newly formed European Space Agency but Gordon believed industry and the universities would grow and develop from the hi-tech research projects the agency would commission.

Ireland joined up and, while it took time for the technological revolution to get the economy into orbit, there are few today who doubt the foresight of those who urged a country lacking in confidence to reach for the stars.

But if it wasn't the scientific arguments that won over the doubters, what was it? "I got good at talking people into doing things they didn't want to do!" Gordon says.

He found himself on the receiving end of that particular skill in 1992 when, at the urging of an acquaintance, he and his wife, Kathleen, went as novices to a meeting of the Irish Guide Dogs for the Blind and left as chairman and secretary. "It was a set-up," Gordon laughs, "and we got caught."

Very quickly, Gordon discovered another vital ingredient to the success of a venture – bravery. From his remove in Sutton, Dublin, he had little idea how precarious the finances of the organisation were at the time. He found out when he joined the board and visited headquarters in Cork soon after.

"We were practically bankrupt but there was great determination. The branches around the country realised the situation was serious and everyone pulled together.

"We got through the worst and then the decision was made that if things were to be done to the best standards, we would need to build a new kennels block and start planning the complete transformation of the buildings into the centre it is today. It took a great deal of courage because we still were not very financially viable but then the Government stepped in with funds and the miracle happened."

Gordon retired from the board in 2006 but not before making his mark by extending the puppy-walking scheme to Dublin.

When not busy with the tasks of chairing his local branch, Gordon loves hill-walking with Kathleen; strolling with their pet labrador, Alex, or taking to the waves with the Howth Sailing and Boating Club.

His own boat is called Ariane after the first rocket launched by the European Space Agency – just as a reminder of what's possible when you aim high.

Gordon Burrows and Alex.

BRIAN BUTLER
Guide dog owner

THE dating game was always tricky but for Brian Butler it took the intervention of the most powerful man in the world to give true love a chance.

"I couldn't go to discos … I might have asked a fella to dance! That might be all right now, but not back then," Brian jokes, recalling a youth spent battling deteriorating eyesight.

Instead of depending on nightclubs for his social life, he took the safer option of joining a Catholic youth group and it was at a peace vigil during the visit of United States President Ronald Reagan to Ireland that he got close to Martina.

"I can't even remember what Reagan was up to at the time - I'm sure he was warmongering somewhere. I kind of forgot about it when I started talking to Martina."

The couple are now married and parents to Clair and Luke but although Martina is Brian's great love, there has been another lady in his life.

Petra was Brian's first guide dog and holds a very special place in his heart. "She was with me when I was living at home. She was there when I lost my sight completely. She was at my wedding. She was there when Clair was born and she was with me when I started college. She shared all the important events in my life."

She didn't live to see Brian graduate, but the moment was glorious nonetheless. As a school-leaver over a decade earlier, he had to give up his science course because he couldn't see well enough.

He worked then for seven years but lost his job when his sight dwindled further. Undeterred, he used the redundancy money to buy a computer and speech software, determined to make himself computer literate for his grand plan of returning to college.

He is now Dr Brian Butler after completing a Bachelor of Arts degree in sociology and history, a masters degree and a PhD. Now tutoring at University College Cork and also working with the college's disability support services, he smiles when he remembers his first terrifying days on campus.

"There were thousands of people milling around and I just thought, how am I going to find the toilets? It was a big decision to make to go back to college and Petra gave me the confidence to do that."

Petra has been followed by Ben and, currently, Isa, both of whom have proved worthy successors.

Brian has the inherited condition, retinitis pigmentosa, although it had not appeared in his family before. Initially it wasn't even suspected as the cause of his sight problems and, as a result, he was 20 years old before he was diagnosed.

It was a blow to discover that Clair had it too but the early discovery has given her and the family time to prepare.

"Clair has a wonderful attitude. People say she must have learned a lot from me but I'm the one who's learnt from her.

"Sometimes I do think this is a bitch - blindness and everything that goes with it - but mostly I just get on with it. There are lots of people out there with perfect sight who are miserable. I have a good life and good things going on for me."

Clair wants to study music and, in a year or two, will start classical voice training. "She has an amazing singing voice. We don't know where she got it from. It's as mysterious as the retinitis pigmentosa. Sometimes good things come out of the blue too."

Brian Butler, wife Martina, daughter Clair, Guide Dog Isa and son Luke.

CLLR CATHERINE BYRNE
Champion of volunteerism

CATHERINE Byrne had to pinch herself when she was handed the keys to the most distinguished address in Dublin city centre.

Brought up in a working class suburb, the city councillor couldn't quite believe she was to live in the Mansion House for a year.

But while dwelling in the Lord Mayor's official residence was an honour, the real privilege of her 2005-2006 term in office was the insight it gave her into every corner of the city and every sector of society living in it.

"When you're made Lord Mayor you're made patron of so many different organisations, but there are ones I'd have a special feeling for. The love of animals drew me to Guide Dogs.

"It was an honour to be patron, even for a year. When you see how much voluntary work is done behind closed doors without recognition, it was nice to say to people that I appreciated what they were doing and that I was saying it on behalf of all the citizens of the city."

Being Lord Mayor meant listening on behalf of all the citizens as well as speaking for them and one of the things Catherine heard was that the city can be a tough place for a person with a disability.

"The city is supposed to facilitate every citizen but there are things out there that are not right. I remember my oldest girl doing a school project where a group of them had to go out in a wheelchair and try to get around for the day, get on a bus, and so on. That evening she was like a raging bull, she was so frustrated.

"You have to put yourself into people's shoes to know what's going on. My father always said if somebody has problems and you can put yourself into their shoes, you're on your way to helping them. That's what I try to do as a public representative."

Catherine loved her time in the Mansion House but she was always a little homesick, not just for familiar things but for the healthy dose of reality that a husband and five children can deliver. "They keep you grounded so you don't get notions. You're just Ma to them."

She did want to leave something behind to mark her year in office, however, so she initiated the Unsung Heroes scheme to recognise voluntary effort.

"It's just a little lapel pin that says you're valued. Our city wouldn't survive without all these people. If all the voluntary people stopped and walked away we would have to get a big key and lock up the island and walk away. It would be worse than a war. It would be turmoil."

JOHN & PATRICK BYRNE
Guide dog owner and long cane user

ONE loves a night out at the pub; the other hates the taste of drink. One loves the bustle of the city; the other can't stand the way no-one there says hello.

John and Patrick Byrne have their differences but as brothers, former work colleagues and now housemates, they have formed a partnership that both of them treasure.

"It works very well but we don't depend on each other. We have our independence," says John. "If I'm going to be late home from the pub, I give him a call. If he's away in Dublin, he phones so I know he's still alive. We're not checking up on each other – we're just being practical."

The bachelor brothers are only a year apart in age and their sight deteriorated simultaneously – the result of an extremely rare blood disorder. A few years ago, they finally had to sell their small farm in Co Mayo and moved into Swinford town.

Around the same time, John was teamed up with guide dog, Quest, and the pair got to know their new neighbourhood together. It was a learning experience both for them and for the town as John is the area's first guide dog owner.

"People would beep the horn to tell you they were letting you across the road but, of course, the dog wouldn't walk out in front of a car, especially one with the horn beeping! People could be too helpful. It took them a while to realise we could get around fine on our own."

John and Quest do a daily tour of the town now and love their surroundings. "Here in Swinford everybody knows you, but you could be in Dublin walking the streets all day long and not a sinner would speak to you."

Patrick, however, loves the city and spends half the week there on a Community Employment Scheme with the National Council for the Blind of Ireland and pursuing computer studies. He hopes to go further and study to be a counsellor.

His work and studies are among the advantages of visual impairment, he says, delighting in knowing that he surprises people by saying there are advantages to having a disability.

"I have come from a situation of no learning two or three years ago, and of barely knowing what a computer was, to studying and doing exams," he explains. "But the real advantage is the people I have met through my work and my studies. I have more of a social life now than I had on the farm and I definitely have more friendship."

Of course, there are disadvantages – one of them being the failure of some sighted people to think before they speak.

"The worst is when people come up to you that you've maybe met only once before and they say: 'Guess who? Go on, guess who I am.' They just don't think. I say the name of someone who's dead or 20 years older than them – just to annoy them! You really need a sense of humour sometimes."

The brothers had to make huge adjustments to their lives while learning to cope with their disappearing sight and both credit Irish Guide Dogs for the Blind with giving them the tools to manage.

"We were each asked separately what routes we needed to cover and what skills we wanted to have," says Patrick. "We were treated as individuals, never just two the same. John and I are chalk and cheese – he's a dog person, I'm not; he's laid back, I'm fiery."

John loves horse racing and showjumping. Patrick is mad about GAA and soccer. Their television schedule rarely clashes but it can be a source of squabbles.

"The only thing we really argue about is the remote control," says John. "You leave it down in the wrong place and there's murder. We spend more time looking for the remote control than anything else. We always find it in the end and swear we'll put it back in the right place next time, but we don't…that's one thing we have in common."

John and Guide Dog Quest.

Pictured overleaf
Patrick in Dublin.

ARLENE CARROLL
Fundraiser

HOSPITAL love stories always sound so romantic but when nurse Arlene Carroll fell for her doctor husband in a busy casualty department, there was little time for daydreaming.

Jimmy took a job as a GP in Carrickmacross in rural south Monaghan and the busy country practice became their way of life.

Arlene remembers many early morning emergencies and long drives on dark nights but, for a pair of blow-ins, there was no better way of integrating into their new community.

"I was the practice nurse so we were both involved. Jimmy worked days as well as every second night, so it was non-stop. It was our life, really. But I love the hands-on type of work and the patient contact. I love that it lets you get to know people."

The 'Doctors on Call' service means the out-of-hours workload is better distributed for GPs across the county now. Arlene works part-time for it, so there is more time for hobbies and she makes the most of it.

She sings with a choir in Drogheda, travelling the country to festivals and competitions, and shyly admits to knowing a tune or two on the piano.

"Jimmy and I are both into sports as well. Squash, tennis, golf, hill-walking – we've done them all but the walking is the favourite." It was through her love of walking and an adored pet golden retriever and occasional show dog called Vicky that Arlene first got involved with Irish Guide Dogs for the Blind.

"Some friends were doing a fundraising dog walk in Dundalk and we went along and they just asked the question could I do something in Carrickmacross. That was it really – 20 years later, I'm still going.

"When I thought about it later, I'd always liked the charity - even from childhood - but I'd kind of forgotten about it. We always had dogs at home in Offaly and my father always said he would love to have a house with 20 dogs and 50 cats. My mother used to say he could have the 20 dogs and 50 cats, but he'd have no wife!"

In a way, Arlene's late father got his wish because, inspired by his daughter's activities, he set up a branch of the organisation in Edenderry.

"He loved the idea that he was helping to provide dogs all over the country and he worked in the post office, so he knew everybody, and it kept him in touch with everyone when he retired.

"That's what I love about it: it keeps you involved with the people around you. You can be an outsider forever in some places but if you really get to know people, you belong."

Arlene Carroll and Polly.

EOIN & MARY CASHMAN
Brood bitch holders and fundraisers

REX was a terrier, had no formal training and lived in an age when guide dogs were barely known; but when it came to looking out for his owner, he was way ahead of his time.

He belonged to Joseph Cashman, who was blind for the last 20 years of his life after losing his sight to glaucoma but who refused to let a lifetime's independence be taken from him.

Joseph died in 1978 but his son, Eoin, and daughter-in-law, Mary, can still picture him heading off from his home near Glanmire in Cork on familiar walks, stick in hand and Rex by his side, both content that they didn't need anyone else's help.

If only the parish priest had been so informed. "One day when Joseph was going to Mass, the parish priest offered to hear his confession any time he would like inside in the house instead of having the trouble of going to the church.

"Well, he was fit to be tied. The idea of it. It was the most insulting thing to him," Mary recalls. "The poor priest was only trying to help but Joseph didn't want help he didn't need.
He didn't want to be treated differently."

Farming and raising a family meant the Cashmans were always busy but when they retired, Eoin suggested offering the use of their outhouses to the Irish Guide Dogs for the Blind breeding programme and before long they had their first expectant mum on their hands.

They have also been puppy walkers and continue to provide a home-from-home for guide dogs whose owners are away. Between the constant new arrivals and their own four dogs, including Betsy, a much-loved labrador, the household is always lively.

Betsy didn't make the grade as a guide dog but she has been an excellent ambassador for the organisation and likes to lend a paw when the Cashmans are fundraising.

Both Mary and Eoin have had their share of ill health but neither lets it get them down. "The dogs make it easier. They're therapeutic. To go out for a walk with them or even just to go and talk to them makes you feel good," Mary says.

Eoin has a similarly positive outlook. He had a hip replacement but has since completed treks in Madeira, Hungary and Slovenia and thought nothing more of tackling the week-long hikes than his father did of rambling along the walks back home.

"I think he would have got have got great use out of a guide dog," says Eoin. "He was very adaptable and very independent. He would have liked not to always have to go on the walks he knew."

BREEDA CLANCY & FAMILY
Fundraisers

SOME families hand down heirlooms, others pass on passions.

The Cotter/Clancy family is a sister act that extends across three generations where Irish Guide Dogs for the Blind is the shared inheritance. Sisters Nora Cotter and Nellie Browne are involved, as are Nora's daughters, Theresa Cotter and Breeda Clancy; and Breeda's daughters, Niamh and Orla.

Breeda is now on the staff working as Regional Development Manager for the southern region, which covers all of Munster. The job involves supporting 34 local branches and all their volunteers, organising fundraisers, devising education and awareness campaigns - and juggling three phone calls at the same time.

"It is non-stop. I started the job seven years ago on April Fool's Day and I often said since, guess who the fool was!"

Humour is never more important than when dealing with the demands of making a serious business fun.

"Getting new people involved in the branches and keeping existing members motivated is very important. A lot of people don't like joining committees - they equate committee with commitment and that scares them because they haven't time for any more commitments.

"Somehow you have to make voluntary work cool and enjoyable and attractive. It is all those things, but getting that message across can be hard. I don't like the word 'committee'. I think 'support group' is a more appropriate description because it's about you giving support when you can, how you can.

"The whole idea of being a volunteer is being able to work it in around the other demands of your life, roping in family and friends to help rather than leaving them on the outside."

Breeda's family lead by example. Her sister Theresa initially roped her in as a volunteer and their mum, Nora, and aunt, Nellie, are the driving forces behind the branch in Mallow, Co Cork.

Ironically, Theresa was petrified when she was approached by a workmate to help out. "I was very shy. I didn't like the idea of going out in public with a collection box at all. You couldn't say boo to me before but now I've become a hard woman to say no to!"

"We have that in common," says Breeda. "I pulled my own daughters in subtly so that they didn't realise they were being sucked in and couldn't say no! It gives them a good sense of community - the idea that you do something and don't always expect to be paid for it. It makes them better adults.

"To be honest, they also enjoy it because every event is a social occasion as well as a good cause. For us, it's also a family occasion, which makes it special too."

From left to right Niamh Clancy, Theresa Cotter, Nellie Browne, Nora Cotter, Breeda Clancy and Orla Clancy

BETHAN COLLINS
Guide dog owner and board member

EVERY bride wants her big day to be unique and Bethan Collins got her wish - her chief bridesmaid had four legs and a tail.

"She was my bridesdog," says Bethan of Nikki, her golden labrador. "Well, the bridesmaid is supposed to be on hand to assist the bride and Nikki certainly fulfilled that duty!"

Walking down the aisle is just one of the adventures Bethan has embarked on. A university lecturer, practising occupational therapist, radio and television presenter and all-round sportswoman, she now combines lecturing with working towards her PhD.

But the young Dubliner with the razor-sharp focus really felt she had reached a high point of accomplishment when she could let her mind wander and her imagination run wild.

For all her other achievements, she can credit her own spirit and determination. For the joy of meandering musings, she thanks Nikki.

"Before I got Nikki, I was using a cane and the concentration required was incredibly demanding. I was going to work trying to picture every step of the way. I was counting paces, remembering where every obstacle was, wondering if the security barrier was up or down. It was almost obsessive, all of this continuous processing of information.

"After I got Nikki I suddenly realised I was daydreaming walking along. Now I can walk with a big grin on my face and my whole body language is so much more relaxed. Being able to daydream is such a luxury. I hadn't realised what I was missing."

Bethan was always visually impaired but her sight deteriorated steadily as she reached her teens, so when it came to choosing a university course after school she had to find one she not only liked but that would lead to a career she could pursue in a practical sense.

"I always wanted to work with people but I knew a blind brain surgeon would not go down so well! I thought about occupational therapy and I did some finding out about it and decided I could do it. It's the philosophy of occupational therapy that I love. It's about enabling people to do the things that they want and need to do in everyday life."

Bethan's first job when she graduated was with the Royal Hospital in Donnybrook, Dublin, where she worked mainly with older people with dementia, stroke survivors and younger people with physical disabilities.

"Nikki was a big hit there. My favourite memory was when I had been up on the ward and came back to find a colleague under the table with Nikki telling her what an awful day he was having. People were very sad when she left. I'm pretty sure they didn't miss me half as much!"

Bethan left after being offered the chance to research her doctorate while lecturing at the School of Occupational Therapy in Trinity College where she herself was taught. But despite her busy schedule, she still took on the job of presenting the RTE Radio series, Audioscope and There's A Good Dog, as well as several television programmes.

She is also a director of Irish Guide Dogs for the Blind and Irish Blind Sports, and she and her husband Michael water-ski and tandem cycle when they get the chance.

"Those are activities I do without Nikki. She's clever but I don't think I'll ever be able to teach her to water-ski! Nikki for me is about doing the everyday things. She's about dignity - the dignity of being able to have a meal with guests in a restaurant and not have to ask one of them to show me to the toilet, of being able to find a bank machine and take out my own money.

"It's important to raise awareness of what guide dogs can do for people because there are a lot of fallacies. You don't need to have no sight whatsoever to get a dog. You don't need to be very old and dependent or very young and fit. You don't need a house with a massive garden and you don't need to be at the end of your tether.

"You just have to want to be yourself. Having Nikki allows me to do the things I want. She lets me be myself."

Bethan Collins with Guide Dog Nikki.

DICK CONNELL
Branch secretary

THE Slieve Bloom Mountains have an enchanting wild beauty that lets them away with the fact that, even by Irish standards, they're not really mountains.

Arderin, the highest peak, proudly translates as the 'Top of Ireland' – though, at just 527 metres tall, it is far from the highest point in the country.

"They're pimples really," says Dick Connell, who knows every rise and fall of the rambling range that spans his own county of Laois and neighbouring Offaly. Yet practising on these modest mounds is taking Dick from the top of Ireland to the top of the world – Nepal.

Every year, Dick, from Portlaoise, organises a sponsored climb of some hilly place in Ireland or Britain for Irish Guide Dogs for the Blind. In 2006, however, the plan was to bring him further and higher. This expedition is organised by Irish Guide Dogs nationally; the destination: the Himalayas.

"They're a bit bigger than we're used to!" says Dick of the 4,000 metre giants that confront him.

Dick found his climbing feet by accident. A transport manager for a waste management company with no more extreme a hobby than breeding cockatiels, he arrived in Galway after a long day's driving around 1986 and stopped at the late John and Patricia Mangan's bed and breakfast.

John was a fellow Laois man and he and Dick got talking. John was very active in Irish Guide Dogs for the Blind and brought Dick to a local meeting. Before Dick knew where he was, he was a founding member of the Laois Support Group.

"I was reluctant to get involved," he admits. "I was just a happy-go-lucky fella who did his own thing. I'd no interest in organisations. But that changed and I changed. I would definitely say life sort of had meaning when I got involved with Guide Dogs."

Dick and the rest of the support group fundraise year-round now with a series of different events, of which the annual climb is just one; and Dick has since begun a separate fundraising campaign for a school in Kenya.

He and his wife Ann were on safari celebrating their 25th wedding anniversary when they came across the children of Zimlati, Mombasa. Dick and the people of Portlaoise have since put a roof on the school and are sponsoring the students' further education.

"When people give to Guide Dogs, they see the benefit for themselves. They see the dogs and know that it gives a blind person independence. In Zimlati people have no jobs and no money but education gives the kids independence. It's a different world but the same principle."

PADDY COYLE
Regional development manager

PADDY Coyle says he can't imagine being chained to a desk – ironic, really, given that he used to sell them for a living.

His transformation from office equipment salesman to development manager with Irish Guide Dogs for the Blind was not only a new career but a whole new way of living.

"It changed my life. When I was selling, I had to create the need in the office for somebody to want a new photocopier or desk or whatever.

"Now, I work in an area of genuine need and genuine service and every cent that's raised through my work, and the volunteers I work with, goes directly towards that service. There is huge job satisfaction.

"I work unsociable hours and travel a lot because you're fitting in with other people's free time which is in the evenings and weekends, but I don't mind. In fact, it has probably helped my social life: when people hear what I am involved in, they want to know more. When I was selling office equipment, it wasn't exactly a conversation starter!"

Dubliner Paddy looks after the North-East for Irish Guides Dogs for the Blind, working with 18 local branches and devising fundraising schemes for the region.

"Every branch is different and the people in them have varied interests, so they go at fundraising from different angles – a coffee morning, a poker classic, a karaoke night – whatever they enjoy.

"Different groups bring in different revenue but you get as much satisfaction from the small cheque as the big one. I use the sporting rule that people should 'play within themselves' – do what they can, do it well, and not compare themselves with others.

"The foundation of our income as an organisation comes from the day-to-day stuff that branches do. Obviously, we love a big donation when it comes; but the counter boxes, the church gate collections, and the local events are what we depend on."

Paddy admits to being totally immersed in the job. He manages a bit of golf and has played a panto dame more than once for a local musical society but work is his main love.

"My wife, Gladys, and I were on holidays touring once and one night in Prague everyone got talking and they perked up when they heard what I do. Before we got on the bus the next morning I had a promise of an invitation to talk to an ICA group and two school visits. You're never away from the work in that sense but you never want to be."

MAGS CREGAN SMART & THE SPECSAVERS STAFF
Sponsors and fundraisers

A COMPETITIVE nature is crucial in business and the staff of Specsavers in Wexford town aim to be the best - both on and off the shop floor.

The colleagues have beaten their co-workers in 29 other Specsavers outlets around the country to raise the most funds for Irish Guide Dogs for the Blind and it's a position they're determined to hold on to.

"My team love to be first at anything they do and they get a kick out of being top of the fundraising table," says the store's co-director, Mags Cregan Smart. "It puts it up to the other stores to try and beat us, and that keeps us all motivated."

Specsavers started in Britain and the company began its involvement with guide dogs charities there too. "They chose Guide Dogs in the UK as their favoured charity and when Specsavers came to Ireland, they brought that commitment with them," Mags explains.

"There needs to be a link with the public beyond the cash register. You're serving them and they're supporting you and that's a very important relationship. The amount of good public relations we get out of doing our little bit for the community is extraordinary."

The staff couldn't help but generate publicity with their antics. During the annual Shades Week fundraising campaign, they ditch their smart uniforms for jeans and tee-shirts, decorate the store with balloons, host broadcasters from the local radio station and "generally harass people on the streets of Wexford for their cash contribution!"

"Very little work gets done," admits Mags, but she and co-director, Steve Schokman, don't mind. "The team have a fabulous time and so do we."

They also run the Women's Mini-Marathon in June each year for the cause. "The guys as well as the girls. The guys dress up as women and it's hilarious."

Nationally during Shades Week, the most coveted raffle prize is a Roy Keane signed jersey but hurling-mad Wexford has its own variation – a purple and gold shirt signed by the senior county hurlers.

"That's something I learned quickly when I came here," smiles British-born Mags. "Everybody wants that shirt!"

Rugby fans aren't forgotten either, especially when Ireland international Gordon D'Arcy is a local hero. "He has helped us out with promotions and he's brilliant," Mags says.

"People like that don't fall in your lap. You have to go and ask. But I'm not one of those people who sits back. If you want things to be done, you have to do them and if you want things to be different, you have to get out and make a difference."

Mags and the
Specsavers Wexford team.

CHARLIE DALY
Chairman, Irish Guide Dogs for the Blind

CHARLIE Daly is never stuck for inspiration.

It comes from the memory of a teacher who taught him the value of giving, from the spirit of endeavour that drives everyone in Irish Guide Dogs for the Blind, and from the support of a family who tell him they're proud.

For Charlie, they have made his demanding role as chairman of the organisation a little less intimidating and a lot more meaningful, a little less exhausting and a lot more fun.

But, even before he was conscious of the important people in his life, another pal was exerting a strong influence: his name was Rascal and he was a border collie.

"My mother died when I was nine years old and my father had died four years before. I prevailed on my aunt Anne O'Connell to get me a dog, and that was Rascal," Charlie recalls. "The bond I had with that dog saw me through some very turbulent times."

Charlie, from Tallow, Co Waterford, and his young siblings, were cared for by relatives and then Charlie was sent as a boarder to St Augustine's College in Dungarvan. He has good memories of the school principal, Fr Moran, who imbued the boys with a sense of giving, but he felt deep loneliness without Rascal by his side.

"When I came back from school on breaks, that dog would be waiting at the top of the boreen for me. He would know I was coming. There was an incredible bond. We were soulmates, basically. It was a latent thing. I didn't have words for it. It was just something that was understood between us."

Years later, when Charlie became involved with Irish Guide Dogs for the Blind, the trust and understanding he saw between guide dog owners and their dogs would often bring Rascal to mind.

The memory also gave Charlie the confidence to press ahead with the pioneering assistance dogs programme for autistic children. "I thought of the bond I had with that dog and that, if only a slight bit of it could transport itself into the relationship between a dog and an autistic child, it could make a difference."

The theory proved correct and the programme's progress has been for Charlie one of the highlights of his three-year term as chairman. "I see it as complementary to our core work – not a change in the organisation but another aspect to it. It's a matter of great pride to me how the organisation had the foresight to embrace a new concept and run with it."

Charlie's 20-plus years of voluntary work with the organisation began when he was already keeping a hectic schedule, working as a legal assistant with Cork County Council by day and studying to become a solicitor at night.

In his scarce spare time, he went on work camps abroad with Voluntary Services International and a canny receptionist at Cork County Hall, Frances Jones, one of the earliest members of Irish Guide Dogs for the Blind, thought her colleague might just like to expend some of his volunteering energies closer to home.

She thought right. Charlie was introduced and his involvement, like the organisation, has grown ever since. He takes great pride in the expanding range and volume of its activities and services.

"For many years we were one of the best kept secrets in Ireland. I like to think that we are no longer so secret."

Selfishness, he insists with a grin, has been his main motivation down through the years. "Pure and utter selfishness. I love it. I get so much out of it. I have had access to some of the best minds around and I have learned more than all the degrees in the world would teach you. I tend to get so wrapped up in it that I wrap other people in as well."

Among those wrapped in are Charlie's wife, Anne, and their three young daughters, Jane, Rachel and Emily. Rufus, Molly and Mr Darcy are the four-legged friends who complete the family.

"The family are amazing in their support. They know I am absolutely passionate about this. That's what it's about: passion. I see it all around me in the organisation. It's incredibly inspiring."

Charlie Daly with wife Ann, Jane aged 12 at the back, Emily aged 8 on left, Rachel aged 10 on the right and Molly and Ruffus.

CLARE DE BURGH
Fundraiser

OLDTOWN in Naas, Co Kildare, has been in the de Burgh family since 1675 when the estate was established by Colonel Thomas Burgh – the architect responsible for Collins Barracks, the original Custom House, and the library at Trinity College, among other noted buildings.

With such an exalted pedigree, it is ironic that the historic holding was better known in modern times for its association with an entirely fictional tycoon.

Clare de Burgh chuckles remembering the fuss when Blake Carrington, oil baron in the television series Dynasty, offered a horse for sale with the proceeds to go to charity.

Of course, the real donor was the actor, John Forsythe, who starred as the millionaire mogul, but the newspapers loved the story and the publicity generated was enormous.

The horse came Clare's way via friends who, like Clare and her husband, John, ran a stud farm. They had the mare in stables for Mr Forsythe and the actor left instructions that the proceeds of her sale should go to a good cause. Clare's friends remembered her involvement with Irish Guide Dogs for the Blind.

"We couldn't afford to advertise Guide Dogs so we said that, whatever price the horse makes, we'll have made an awful lot already in publicity."

Clare's work with Irish Guide Dogs for the Blind began with her late labrador, Beau, a name that turned out to be appropriate. The organisation was starting its breeding programme and needed good stock to begin a dynasty of its own. "I was very honoured they chose Beau. He sired a lot of litters."

Clare went on to start a branch of the organisation locally and became an avid fundraiser with the mantra: Always say thank you. "I am a great believer in saying thank you. And I mean it from the bottom of my heart because I am so grateful for what people do."

She had an early opportunity to say thank you as a young wife and mother-to-be in 1955 when the wing of the residence she and John were about to move into burned down.

"The men and boys of Naas rescued all the furniture through the windows. The roof was burning and the ceiling was falling in on them and they wouldn't get out until they had rescued practically everything. We were so grateful."

The famous estate has now been sold and Clare and John will be moving out, severing the de Burgh ties with the property forever, but Clare is philosophical. "It is a little sad but one of our sons has built a home in Co Wicklow and called it Oldtown, so a new history will begin there. I hope it's as interesting as the one we've known."

SHEILA DELANEY & EILEEN O'RIORDAN
Fundraisers and puppy walkers

IT takes something special to create a traffic jam in Kilmurray on an average day but two women can take pride in bringing the quiet Co Cork village to a standstill once a year.

Sheila Delaney and Eileen O'Riordan are chief organisers of the annual Poulanargrid Harriers show in aid of Irish Guide Dogs for the Blind and, after 22 years, the event is as much an institution in the area as the Harriers Club itself.

The entire community gets involved in baking cakes, arranging flowers, organising raffles, supplying music, erecting stalls and setting up side-shows. The crowds are so big that the local GAA club has to provide stewards for traffic management.

Everyone in the Harriers Club loves dogs, so Irish Guide Dogs for the Blind was a natural choice as their adopted charity. As soon as the harrier season ends in March, attention turns to the show and an organising committee meets weekly under gaslight in the ageing mobile home that serves as clubhouse.

"It's great to have it. We've no toilet in it, but that keeps the meetings short and to the point!" says Sheila.

If anyone is in doubt about the benefit their efforts bring, they need look no further than fellow member, Eileen, who has been a puppy walker for 27 years. She can't recall a time when she didn't have a pup arriving as a floppy, fluffy six-week-old and leaving as a robust one-year-old ready for training as guide dog.

"It's hard to see them go. The new owner will write and thank you and you get sent cards at Christmas - from the dogs as well as the owners. But I wouldn't want to see them. You leave them off to do the best they can, and that's it."

Puppy walking requires commitment, but Eileen also has three pet dogs and 14 harriers so she doesn't notice an extra tail. Sheila, meanwhile, is kept busy with four jack russells, a cocker spaniel and six harriers.

The friends have known each other since childhood although they came to harriers by different routes. Sheila's family always had harriers and her husband, Tim, enjoys lending a hand, while Eileen jokes that her involvement was a condition of marriage to Donal, the club chairman.

Outside of harrier season, the two women go on regular rambles through the woods while the dogs enjoy a summer break and dream of a return to action in November.

"I love the outdoor life," says Eileen. "I go away for fine walks and it costs me nothing." Sheila is equally baffled by people who spend money to exercise. "All the people going to gyms to keep well, and if you go to a doctor in the morning he will tell you to take a walk!"

"They'd be better saving their money - and giving it to Guide Dogs."

Back row left to right Shane McCarthy, Dermot Mac Sweeney, Dermot O'Mahoney, Donal O'Riordan, Conor Calaghan, Tommy Murray, Jerry Mac Sweeney. Front row Michael Galvin, Theresa O'Leary, Sheila Delaney, Eileen O'Riordan, John Murphy.

JIM & PAT DENNEHY
Co-founder and president, and supporter

JIM Dennehy never intended to be a crusader.

With a young family, his own flourishing car business, and a reputation as a fine amateur rugby player, his life was full and the future was packed with promise.

It was 1968 and he was the proud father of a second baby daughter just two days old when he was rushed to casualty. The shooting accident that took his sight was so serious that nuns were dispatched to the maternity ward to break the news to his unsuspecting wife, Pat, that he was not expected to survive.

He beat the odds but his return to health was just one step on the long journey he had to take to regain his way of life.

"The total loss of sight was immediate and traumatic," says Jim. "But the shock was further compounded when I learned that there was no mobility training of any kind in Ireland.

"I was finally knocked for six when a senior medical consultant told me I'd be of great help to my wife in our home! I felt I was being condemned to a life sentence as a prisoner in my home. But, rather than becoming demoralised, I pledged to prove the consultant wrong."

Jim entered a rehabilitation training centre in Torquay, England, where he learned to use a long cane, but he also put himself on a waiting list with British Guide Dogs for the Blind, which eventually provided him with his first guide dog.

He left Torquay energised and optimistic but also angered that there were no similar facilities in Ireland. "I pledged that when I returned to Ireland I would move heaven and earth to have a mobility training centre established."

He made contact with fellow Cork resident, Mary Dunlop, already well known for her fundraising work for British Guide Dogs, and she quickly fell in with his mission.

The Department of Health was sympathetic to their campaign but said there was insufficient need to warrant specialist services for the blind. The Cork duo vowed to convince them otherwise and organised a series of regional conferences in an attempt to gauge demand. The campaign culminated in a national meeting in the Mansion House in 1975 where there was standing room only for much of the attendance.

As a result, the Irish Guide Dog Association, as it was then called, was formed in 1976 and a small training centre was set up in Dublin before moving to its current location at Model Farm Road in Cork in 1979.

"We trained our first two dogs in 1980 and since then we've gone from strength to strength," says Jim. "But none of this would have been achieved without the fantastic support from our volunteers and staff. They have performed heroically through the good and difficult times."

And there were tough times. One Christmas there wasn't enough money in the bank to pay the wages beyond January. As they stared into the abyss, a bequest of £250,000 suddenly arrived from an animal lover in Waterford.

"I said I would have moved heaven and earth," says Jim, "but I think heaven played a fair part!"

The organisation was almost a full-time job in itself but Jim also resumed his position at the helm of his business and he marked 50 years as a Ford dealer at Dennehy's Cross in Cork in 2006.

He has had four guide dogs and one in particular was a bonus to the business. The dog hated raised voices and when he got upset broke wind of the most pungent kind. "It meant that any boardroom disagreements had to be sorted out without shouting. It made us all very civil!"

Jim loves travel and intends that he and Pat will do much more of it when he retires, which he is now happy to do as he believes he has finally achieved enough to bury the gloomy predictions of the doom-laden consultant from all those years ago.

"Maybe I should have gone from the business sooner but you forget your age when you don't see yourself in a mirror. My wife and family haven't aged either. Their faces are still the same to me as they were in 1968."

IRENE DILLON
Fundraiser

RENE Bourke's Swing Quartet played dance halls all over the country in the early 1960s, the eponymous Rene belting out popular hits on piano and accordion.

Cities like Galway and Limerick, towns like Wexford and Donegal, villages like Miltown Malbay and Glenties – Irene lists the venues as if she was still using the name Rene and preparing to tour.

It amazes even herself to realise she hasn't been away from home for over 40 years. Her last holiday was her honeymoon. "I could go away for the day but not overnight," she says firmly. "I couldn't leave the dogs."

Irene was brought up with dogs. Her father was a tailor, running his business next to the Carlow town house where she still lives, but he also bred Irish wolfhounds. "I was an only child and the dogs were family to me," she says.

It was heartbreaking for her when her father's sight began to fail and he had to give up tailoring and go to England to find work. When he left, the wolfhounds had to go too.

She remembers him returning to Ireland when his condition worsened and how he lived his last 10 years without sight. "He came to terms with it, but there was no such thing as guide dogs then. He would have been a natural with a guide dog, he knew so much about dogs."

Irene followed him into business, setting up a hairdressing salon in his old tailor's shop and although she gave it up when she married Tommy Dillon, she never forgot the other interest she had shared with her father - dogs.

Tommy gave her a cocker spaniel for their 21st wedding anniversary and soon Irene was winning awards at shows. She began breeding Cavalier King Charles spaniels and still has five of the thick-maned creatures, which she jokes are the only curly heads of hair she grooms now.

Through the dogs, she became involved in Irish Guide Dogs for the Blind and she only retired in 2006 after 26 years of non-stop committee work and fundraising.

She hasn't given up her community work, though. Now widowed, she devotes her time to her dogs and to running messages for the sick and elderly in the locality. It is the kind of caring that won her a Carlow Person of the Year Award for humanitarian work in 2000, although she dismisses the idea that she is anything extraordinary.

"When I was in the dance band and when I was hairdressing, I was always meeting people," she explains. "I just like being mixed up with people."

Irene Dillon with Bobbi, Carol Lawler – Millard with Lady Di.

MELANIE & JOHN DOLAN
Guide dog trainer and Guidelines editor

THERE isn't much that goes on at Irish Guide Dogs for the Blind that John and Melanie Dolan don't know about.

If Melanie hasn't trained the dog at the National Headquarters and Training Centre in Cork, then John has written about the owner in the organisation's quarterly magazine and, as often as not, they've crossed paths with both.

They can even thank dogs for crossing their romantic paths. Melanie, from Leixlip, Co Kildare, had a childhood friend whose mum had a guide dog. Angela Allen and her dog, Kara, were a formidable pair and the young Melanie was fascinated by them.

"Angela and Kara were my first introduction to guide dogs and that stayed with me. My background is science and I was working in a lab in Sligo when I just decided I didn't want to do it anymore. I wanted to work with animals."

Melanie moved to England to do a specialist animal care course and went into kennel work. It was during her time there that she met John who was working for a London newspaper.

Their decision to make a home in Ireland with their little son Joshua proved a good one – for guide dogs as well as the Dolans. Melanie got a job as a guide dog trainer and John became features editor at the Evening Echo newspaper but also began editing Guidelines from home in his spare time.

"The magazine is very important for keeping members in touch with each other and with the dogs. A puppy walker loves to see the dog they had featured with their new owner, and volunteers like to read what fundraisers and other events are going on," he says.

"I do a lot of interviews with people who have guide dogs and the way they go about managing their disability never ceases to amaze me. In my job I deal with a lot of showbusiness types and public relations people but the people I speak to for Guidelines are a bit left-field. There's something very compelling about them."

Melanie meets a lot of fascinating characters too – a lot of them the four-legged kind.
"My work begins when the puppy walkers finish. We get the bouncy, silly pups and turn them into mature, well-behaved dogs ready for intensive guide dog training.

"Every one of them is different but I actually like the cheekier ones. You need an awful lot of patience but it really is worth it when the naughty pup becomes an obedient dog."

"We're in a privileged position," says John. "Melanie sees the organisation from the dog's point of view and I see it from a people perspective. Unfortunately, I can't interview the dogs but at least I can get an idea what they're thinking!"

John and Melanie, son Joshua and Merlin.

FRANK DOWNES
Chairman, Galway branch

WHEN Frank Downes sits at the end of his road, waiting for a break in the endless stream of traffic and wondering if he'll ever get a chance to pull out, he feels impatience stirring inside.

But then he remembers how things used to be and he's happy to wait.

Frank left Ireland as a boy when his family emigrated to England and he returned at a time when many like him were heading in the opposite direction. As a sales rep for Claddagh Minerals driving around the towns and villages of Galway, he saw entire communities emptying before his eyes.

"I called to one pub in the early eighties and the owner was very down. A busload of men had gone out to England that morning because there was no work and he said the man up the street had taken 14 of his customers that year ... 'the man up the street' was an undertaker."

Places that, back then, were fast becoming ghost towns are buzzing with life now, including Frank's own village of Moycullen where the traffic to and from Galway city is non-stop.

"It's fantastic to see villages alive again. It's great for older people. When there are things going on around you, it encourages you to stay active."

Staying active was a priority for Frank when he took early retirement in 2004 but he needn't have worried about turning into a couch potato. After 25 years of involvement in Irish Guide Dogs for the Blind, he knows how to keep busy.

"I play golf a couple of days a week, I do a bit of DIY and help with the garden, and Ollie, who's a retired guide dog, keeps me occupied; but Guide Dogs really keeps me going. You couldn't put enough time into it if there were two of you. I wish there were two of me or I wish I could win the Lotto so I could give them a massive cheque."

Frank felt like he had won the Lotto in 2006 when two surprise honours came his way to mark his contribution to the Irish Guide Dogs for the Blind.

He received a Galway Person of the Year award and he was duped by friends into joining the audience of the television programme, When Dreams Come True, only to find out that the spotlight was on him. He was presented with a dream trip to Canada to meet up with friends he and his wife, Mary, had not seen since 1969.

"I was so overwhelmed, I could feel the tears coming. You don't want thanks. The thanks go to the public for supporting us. I just want to be useful – that's reward enough."

Frank Downes with Ollie.

MARGARET DUCKER
Brood bitch holder and puppy walker

ODD though it sounds, it was a rabies scare that introduced Margaret Ducker to one of the most enjoyable phases of her life.

Irish Guide Dogs for the Blind had not yet started its own breeding programme and was still taking pups from England, so when travel restrictions were signalled after a rabies outbreak on mainland Europe, the organisation looked around for advice.

There weren't too many vets in Co Cork who had experience of rabies but Margaret's husband, David, had worked in Central Africa, now Malawi, and soon found his phone ringing.

Margaret and her late husband met in Africa in the 1950s where she had gone to teach when barely out of school herself. "I suppose it was quite adventurous for a young woman at the time," she says with understatement.

The next adventure she and David would share was perhaps less exotic, but no less thrilling. "We reared five children and 115 pups!"

At one point they had 19 pups in the house, born in two litters a week apart, and a system of sharp eyes and baby-gates had to be put into place to stop them getting mixed up as their world expanded gradually from the confines of the whelping box to the kitchen, the porch, the yard and finally the garden.

It meant a recurring round of all-night watches on birthing mums, dawn choruses of hungry yelps, and constant alertness for the pup who might or might not be under your feet.

"People often said how could you bear to see them go but I said, very easily – we're exhausted! But that was the story of our life for 18 years. David and I had some great times and I can look back and say we shared it.

"It's a great way to bring up children and what you learn from bringing up children applies to rearing pups. What you learn as a child influences you later in life, especially if you have learnt to be afraid. Our job was to make sure the pups were not afraid. I hope we did that with our children and we certainly tried to do it with the pups."

Margaret's motto is always to challenge fear. She is an avid member of the Irish Countrywomen's Association and also teaches oil painting classes and she likes to encourage others not to be shy about using their talents or hold back because they are nervous of what others might think.

"Other people's opinions are worth listening to but that means your opinion counts too and if you don't listen to yourself, who else is going to pay any heed?"

MICHAEL DUFFY
Branch chairman

FROM his years in the theatre Michael Duffy knows that the members of the backstage crew are just as important as those who appear front of house.

The analogy applies equally well to his voluntary work with Irish Guide Dogs for the Blind over the last quarter of a century, during which time he has never failed to be amazed and heartened by the good deeds performed by people who seek no limelight or applause.

"An old lady called me up and said she had jam money in the credit union she wanted to give me so she could sponsor a guide dog pup because her husband had been blind before he died," Michael recalls.

"I didn't know what she meant – I thought maybe she had coins collected in a jam jar. But I went with her as she asked and we left the credit union with a cheque for €7,500 she raised from making jam for the local shop. There are people like that toiling away behind the scenes all over this country that you never hear about."

They exist further afield than Ireland, too. One stalwart supporter lives in Abu Dhabi in the United Arab Emirates and rallies the Irish community there to run fundraisers for the organisation.

"It keeps them in touch with home. They don't feel they're missing out so much when they're doing something that has a direct benefit back home."

Home for Michael is Athlone, Co Westmeath, where he is well known not just for Irish Guide Dogs for the Blind, but also long years of voluntary work with the Irish Society for the Prevention of Cruelty to Animals and the local musical society.

Athlone Musical Society is the oldest in Ireland, celebrating its centenary in 2002, and, like a popular show, it just keeps running. Its annual shows are massive extravaganzas that enjoy packed houses every night.

"We have all these new entertainment forms now – iPods and DVDs and wide-screen televisions – but technology hasn't killed the joy of a life stage performance."

Michael's role is behind the curtain, although he will fill a gap in the chorus if needed. Retired from work and widowed since the loss of his wife, Ann, in 2005, he spends the rest of his spare time enjoying bridge, rugby, GAA, soccer and gardening; stewarding at Knock Shrine, and pampering his Norwegian elkhound.

Irish Guide Dogs for the Blind gets priority over them all, however. "It's the inspiration of the people who we help that keeps you doing it. Sometimes it's hard because organising and motivating people is hard. You wouldn't dine out on it but then it's not done for the glory, just for the good."

ALAN DUKES
Board member

ALAN Dukes had big plans for when he retired from politics.

He would do some consultancy work, visit every Norman castle in the country, and spend a year in the Rocky Mountains chronicling the changing seasons. He dreamed he might even repeat the experience in north-western China.

But politics had another plan for him. In one of the shocks of the 2002 general election, he lost his seat in Kildare South. After 21 years in the Dail, during which he led Fine Gael for three years and was minister four times, suddenly Leinster House was no longer home.

Coming to terms with the disappointment of defeat, Alan decided he had better fast-forward his retirement plans and began work as a consultant on Eastern European affairs. He then got the job of director of the Institute of European Affairs and juggled both roles. In the middle of the juggling act, he was taken on as a consultant with a public relations firm.

Not surprisingly, he hasn't seen the Rockies yet, nor the Norman castles, and China is looking increasingly remote. "I'm not complaining," he says, listing the five countries his work will take him to in the next four months. "I'm doing work that I love."

It says much about the persuasive powers of Irish Guide Dogs for the Blind that the organisation managed, firstly, to track down their globetrotting target; and, secondly, to get him on the board.

"They wanted someone who knew their way around the political system, who could deal with the official agencies and who would give them an outsider's view on what was going on in the organisation – someone who would be naturally sceptical. I was a cynical politician for 21 years, so I was well qualified on that count."

As a TD, Alan knew constituents who had trouble accessing disability services but it was his late father, Jim, who came to mind when he began learning about the work of Irish Guide Dogs for the Blind.

"For a good many years before he died, my father was involved with the Irish Wheelchair Association. He'd had a stroke and he was depressed because he couldn't drive. But we got the car modified and he re-sat the driving test and it gave him back his freedom. That gave me a better awareness of the importance of giving people their mobility."

Since he joined, Alan has helped plan the future of Irish Guide Dogs for the Blind so that it can fulfill its ambitions of increasing the number of dogs it produces, the services it offers, and the clients it helps.

"There's a lot of work to be done but it has been an eye-opener. As a politician, you think you've seen it all but I've found out otherwise."

MICHAEL EDMONDS
Breeding and puppy walking supervisor

THE arrival of each new litter of guide dog puppies seems like a simple journey from Mother Nature straight to the human heart. But the oohs and aahs of enchanted delight disguise a highly sophisticated and scientific behind-the-scenes operation.

"We're breeding the equivalent of a superhuman," says Michael Edmonds. "We can't leave anything to chance."

The breeding programme of Irish Guide Dogs for the Blind has to plan three years ahead to meet the needs of new guide dog owners as well as existing clients needing successors for retiring dogs, and quality can never be sacrificed for quantity.

"When the pups are born, they're with their mother for six weeks; then they are taken, separated and placed into adopted homes. After 10 months they come to the kennels for a while and then they go to the training centre and, finally, to a guide dog owner.

"All this happens in the first year-and-a-half of the dog's life. For that dog to succeed, it has to be of fantastic character, amazing temperament, very rounded and very versatile. You and I would have been broken mentally by such dramatic changes – the dog not only has to cope, but has to perform brilliantly."

Yet when Michael joined Irish Guide Dogs for the Blind in 1983, he was a carpenter by trade whose only experience of animal husbandry was his own pet labrador giving birth.
That was more experience than most applicants for the breeding supervisor position, however, so Michael got the job. "You'd laugh if I applied for the same job now. But back then we were all finding our feet and we had to start somewhere."

With the support of the British guide dogs organisation, Michael had some labrador bitches mated and the Irish breeding programme began. Trial, error and crossed fingers have been replaced by the science of cytology, or cell analysis, as well as intricate screening, scanning, matching and monitoring.

Currently the programme works at a rate of mating a bitch, delivering a litter and placing a set of siblings with puppy walkers at least once a month, and the goal is to double up on everything.

The programme has also produced experimental labrador-poodle and labrador-Burmese mountain dog mixes which may have additional physical and personality traits useful to working dogs.

"We're learning more all the time," says Michael. "People often say isn't it a pity we can't breed humans as good! I say we don't need to – they're already out there, our volunteer brood bitch holders and puppy-walkers. They're the unsung heroes. We do the science and they do the loving and caring. It's a great combination."

Michael with Brood Bitch Golden Retriever Vicky, and Brood Bitch German Shepard Zoe.

ALISON & ROGER FLACK
Puppy walker and board member

ROGER Flack had just one rule when wife, Alison, became a puppy walker for Irish Guide Dogs for the Blind: any pup living under his roof had to be black.

Roger didn't like dogs and he especially didn't like the idea of white hairs all over his good business suits. At least black would blend in.

The rule was religiously observed – for a while. But rules bend and mindsets change. To Roger's ongoing amazement, he not only conceded to a succession of fair-haired creatures sharing his living space, but he also became chairman of the organisation.

"He only has himself to blame," says Alison, who recalls how, as the mother of three children under the age of five, she complained that she needed an interest to give her something to talk about "other than piddling children".

"Roger saw a notice looking for puppy walkers and said now you can talk about piddling puppies instead!"

Over the next 23 years, Alison's interest was to become a family passion. Roger, a chartered surveyor and a director of estate agents Hamilton Osborne King, was asked for his advice when the organisation began making plans to upgrade its facilities.

"At the time they were in the old farmhouse and the buildings were long past their sell-by date," he says, recalling an estate agent's nightmare. "The house was on three different levels, it had narrow corridors and low ceilings, and the heating didn't work. The kennels were all breezeblock and corrugated iron and were too hot in summer and too cold in winter. The site was good enough to keep but everything else had to go."

The building programme was ambitious and, as time went on, Roger became more and more involved, joining the board and serving a term as chairman. "It's been a terrific challenge and I've really enjoyed it. I was pleased to be asked to help. Estate agents are not high on peoples' credibility list, so it's nice to be able to give something back!"

Alison, meanwhile, is chairperson of the vibrant Rochestown branch of the organisation in the couple's adopted Cork city. Their latest fundraiser is a re-issue of their 20-year-old cookbook in which 1980s celebrities give their favourite recipes. The first is contributed by US President Ronald Reagan, who revealed a passion for macaroni cheese.

The couple's son and two daughters have also become great supporters of the organisation and son Jonathan is doing the 2006 Nepal trek to raise funds. Roger still doesn't regard himself as a true doggy person, but he knows when he's outnumbered.

"I gave in years ago," he laughs. "Alison knew she'd won when I got her a badge that says: "Love is…letting her keep her big hairy dog!"

Roger and Alison with Guide Dog Puppy Viv.

MARTIN GORDON
Guide dog owner

IF life was fair, Arsenal wouldn't lose a Champions League final, a pint wouldn't cost more in Dublin, and Martin Gordon wouldn't have gone blind at the age of 17.

Some injustices you have to accept, but others are just looking for a fight - and Martin feels fired up to take them on.

Since starting his law and politics degree at National University of Ireland, Galway, in 2004, Martin has developed a passion for human rights law and, although he finds the theory of politics more inspiring than the practice, he believes he could get angry enough to run for election some day.

If he did, he would make disability issues a key part of his platform. "Do you know there is no article in the Constitution about people with disabilities?" he asks. "There's an assumption everyone is the same. We'd all like to be treated the same, but sometimes that means making special provision for some people.

"There are very few incentives for people with disabilities to go to college, for example. There should be a certain number of places reserved for students with disabilities, or greater flexibility around the entry requirements. It just takes some people longer to get the points than students without disabilities. It doesn't mean they're any less able for the course.

"I'm not a quiet fellow. I'll ask when I need something and I'll push to get it. But what about all the quiet people? They just get left in the dark. They need someone to push for them."

Martin had continuous eye trouble as a child but when he went completely blind overnight at 17 the impact was devastating.

"Everything was going through my head. Thoughts like: Am I going to continue at school? Where do I go from here? Will my life continue or will it stop? One of the first things I was clear about was wanting to get to university, so I said right - now I have to get back to school."

He spent the summer break training to use a long cane and returned to class fully mobile. "I had to get my independence," he says. "There was no way I was going to be led by the hand anywhere." Rugby and soccer were huge parts of his life and it was hard to go from competitor to spectator but he filled the gap with rowing, swimming, the gym and even the occasional rock climb.

He was determined not to be left on the sideline where his academic pursuits were concerned, either. With a third level institution on his doorstep in his hometown of Sligo, Martin might have been expected to stay locally, but his heart was set on Galway.

"Initially it was daunting. You think, right so I'm adult now - there are no clean clothes and the cupboards are empty. Help!"

The university has given Martin any help it can, including a personal assistant. "He's a Spurs supporter and I'm an Arsenal supporter, but apart from that we get on great!"

Martin also did an independent living skills course with Irish Guide Dogs for the Blind to equip himself with tips for cooking and household chores. But the greatest help of all is Jake, a gregarious giant of a labrador who is equally at home in the buzz of the college bar as he is in the hush of the library. Martin reckons he deserves at least an honorary degree on graduation day.

"It's not just the practicalities of getting around. He opens so many doors in other ways. People respond so well to him that they don't shy away from me. I was lucky in that I knew people going to college but I've made other friends besides. Jake gives me a freedom I couldn't imagine otherwise."

Martin's message to other young people is not to let a disability deter them from their dream. "I'd just say: get up and go. You can't stay at home forever and when you make the move, you don't look back."

He hopes he doesn't have to move too far to get a job, though. "I'm really proud to be from the West. Besides, I wouldn't be able to afford a hangover in Dublin!"

Martin with Guide Dog Jake.

LENA GOURLEY
Guide dog owner

LENA Gourley has enjoyed her share of street entertainment without ever having to put a coin in a busker's cap.

She recalls how two women once stopped behind her and her guide dog, Shauna, at a pedestrian crossing and began a running commentary on her every move.

Before the lights had changed, Lena had learned that she was a "poor afflicted woman" who was stone deaf, bad with her nerves, suffering from poor circulation, and unlikely to live long.

She was so entertained by this version of her apparently appalling existence that she never let on she could hear every word and was intrigued when the women decided to follow her around to see how she managed.

"I thought I better tell them but then I said, no, I'll not spoil the plot. I don't know how I didn't burst. I was hysterical trying not to laugh."

When she called into the vet's to pick up ear drops and mineral powders for Shauna, the women knew their diagnosis was correct.

"'You see,' one said to the other, 'she's getting a bottle of drops for her hearing and powder for her blood.' They didn't even see it was the vet they were at, not the doctor!"

Lena, born up the hill on Cork's northside, a stone's roll from the city centre, didn't have time to prepare for losing her sight or for the sometimes comically ill-informed attitudes some people would have towards her.

"I went to bed perfectly able to see and woke up in the morning blind," she says matter-of-factly. Her retinas had both become detached without explanation overnight and surgery to reattach them failed.

It was 1977 and Lena was 30 years old and a full-time carer for her much younger siblings and an elderly neighbour. She couldn't imagine a life relying on someone else to care for her so she made it a mission to find out how she could win her freedom back.

When she learned that Irish Guide Dogs for the Blind was planning to train dogs in Cork, she immediately applied. There were five long years to wait but eventually she became part of the group of four who were the first Irish people to receive an Irish-trained guide dog.

"I got Shauna and life began again. There was no road too big to travel. I went back to looking after my neighbour and then I looked after my mother and we never needed any help. People would say to my mother, how are you getting on looking after that daughter of yours and she would say, sure I'm not doing anything – Lena looks after me.

"You see, blindness is not a handicap when you have a dog. With a dog you have mobility and a friend for life. You can get around like anyone else and people who know you forget that you can't see.

"Older people sometimes don't understand in the way younger people do. Blind children are integrated into normal schools now and it gives the sighted children an insight into blindness.

"They see blind people are the same as anyone else only they can't see. I can function now as a sighted person. I do all my own messages. I can go anywhere in the city just by saying the place to the dog. I've been to England visiting on my own. Isn't that great for a person that's so afflicted!"

Lena was entertained again on a more recent trip into the city centre when she came out of the English Market with her current dog, Judy, and an elderly woman asked for help getting down the steps because she didn't see well.

She then asked to be helped across the road and remarked that Lena was great, training in dogs for the poor blind people.

"'God bless and spare you that you never want for one yourself,' she said. Then she asked me to tell her when the number three bus was coming. I said I was sorry but I had to get the dog back to the centre before it closed. She never knew otherwise and that's the way I like it."

Lena with Guide Dog Judy.

DR TERRY GRIMES
Consultant veterinary ophthalmologist

NO human can claim to truly have a dog's eye view of the world but Dr Terry Grimes comes close.

The country's only veterinary surgeon specialising full time in ophthalmology, he has been peering into the eyes of guide dogs for 30 years in a bid to ensure their sight really is good enough to see for two.

"We still don't know exactly how the dog sees the world. We believe his ability to see in colour is quite limited and he is essentially a wild animal, so his eye is developed mainly to pick out movement, but we have no concept of how much is added by his sense of smell – how much he 'sees' with his nose.

"We can't make a dog read a chart on the wall so our observations are quite crude compared to a human ophthalmologist. But we don't seem to do that bad a job."

In the experience of Irish Guide Dogs for the Blind, the job done is extremely good. Terry travels at regular intervals to the National Headquarters and Training Centre in Cork where he gives his services free of charge, examining pups, brood bitches, trainees and working guide dogs for any sign of trouble.

"If a dog develops eye problems, he won't complete the full seven or eight years of a guide dog's working life and he may present a danger to the owner so we try to avoid a situation where problems will arise.

"Another way we're trying to avoid difficulties is through the breeding programme. A lot of pedigree dogs are prone to hereditary problems – glaucoma, cataracts, diseases of the retina and optic nerve – and if we can pick them out early, we can make sure they don't go into the breeding stock."

Terry also treats any guide dog which develops a problem that is beyond the experience of the local vet. He arrived from London in 1967 and has worked at University College Dublin ever since, teaching and treating at the veterinary hospital, to which animals are referred to benefit from the collective expertise on hand.

On an average day, the cages, pens and yards can house anything from a turtle to a bull while the stables cater for an array of ponies and horses. While some of his patients are impressive in size, Terry loves the minute intricacies of the eye and is grateful for the chance to specialise in his chosen field.

He actually retired in late 2005 but hasn't given up setting his alarm clock yet. "They asked me to come back and do lectures and clinics and surgery. I must have been retired all along at that rate! But I'm glad to do it because I love it. It's a hobby as well as a job. How many people can say that?"

MARY HARNEY
Minister for Health and Children

RUNNING the most demanding government department with the biggest State budget doesn't faze Minister Mary Harney but just ask her to remember her glasses and she instantly admits defeat.

"I used to wear glasses but I can't be trusted with them. I'd be forever losing them, leaving them down somewhere and walking out without them so that I wouldn't be able to work for the day," she confesses. "For the sake of my job, I can't wear them."

Ideally, she needs bifocals but instead, with the pragmatism of a seasoned politician, she wears one contact lens so she can see long distance and leaves the other eye free for reading. "It's probably an unusual solution but it works!"

Minister Harney has long known the importance of eye health. Glaucoma runs in her family and she and her close relatives must have regular check-ups – a point brought home to her when her late uncle, Tom Harney, lost his sight to the condition in the late 1990s.

"To lose your sight when you have had it all your life is very traumatic. Uncle Tom got great solace from the radio. He lived in Chicago but he would listen to an Irish programme that had all the political news from Ireland. He never missed that so he would always know what I was up to."

If Minister Harney learned about blindness from her uncle, she learned about disability in general from her dear mother, Sarah, who suffered a stroke in 1993 and has had to cope with the physical impact as well as losing much of her speech.

"I discovered people perceive you differently when you have a disability. If we are in a restaurant, the staff tend to talk to my mother through me. That's not good. You learn a lot when you are close to someone who has disabilities. You learn how to normalise life as much as you can because that's what everyone wants – a normal life."

It is the ability of Irish Guide Dogs for the Blind to do just that – normalise life – that so impresses the minister, and her impressions are important as State funding makes up just under 20pc of the organisation's annual budget and most of that comes through the Department of Health and its agencies.

"Instead of focusing on the difficulties and challenges, they focus on abilities and independence so that people can live as normally as possible. They're helping people, not feeling sorry for them; rather than the 'victim' approach, it's the 'ability' approach.

"One of the projects I was very taken with was the assistance dogs programme for children with autism. I think that is smashing. It's a very innovative organisation. I'd like them continue being innovative and coming forward with new ideas and I'd like to see that we could support that."

While Irish Guide Dogs for the Blind celebrates its 30th year, Minister Harney is just one year off that personal milestone, as she first entered Leinster House as a senator in 1977 before being elected as a TD four years later.

After three decades in politics, she says she still continues to learn new things and one of her most valuable lessons – apart from giving up on glasses – came to her only in very recent years.

"I learned you have to have space away from the everyday activity of politics. It's only in the last couple of years that I have taken reasonable holidays. It is so important to recharge the batteries and clear the head.

"Even during the everyday business, you need to take time out. I like Scrabble and crosswords and I'm hooked on Sudoku – I can't go to bed at night leaving a puzzle unfinished. My husband, Brian, is a good cook so it's great to be able to sit down to a meal together. They're just normal things but they're important."

ED HARPER
Guide dog owner

ED Harper is plotting a rebellion over on Cape Clear. Battling bureaucracy emanating from Brussels is not easy when you're an island dweller off the south-west coast of Ireland, far removed from the corridors of power, but Ed's war-cry is: Come and get me.

Ed took it on the chin when new European Union food production regulations stopped him sending his specialist goats' cheeses by post to restaurants and delicatessens on the mainland. He had to cut his milking herd by two-thirds and the drop in income almost ruined him, forcing him to rebuild a precarious existence by selling his produce to the small population of islanders and the visitors who come during the short tourist season.

But he is refusing point-blank to go along with a new directive ordering goat owners to tag their animals' ears.
His goats have long, soft, delicate ears and he says the regulation tags will tear the thin skin, catch in briars, trap the animals and prevent them lifting and moving their lobes to send signals to the rest of the herd.

"They say it's for traceability because of BSE, but if they're so concerned they could use microchips. We already hand over goat carcasses for BSE testing so we're not opposed to testing but no farmer concerned about the welfare of his goats is going to tag them, and no farmer with an untagged goat is going to hand it over for testing because he'll be found to be against the law. Well, that just means even less BSE monitoring than before.

"They can try to force me if they want but they'll have to come to the island and do it themselves. I'd like to see them try to round up my goats!"

Ed has never actually seen a goat. Blind since infancy, the Manchester-born academic and folk singer discovered the animals through some small-time goat breeders he met in a folk group in the 1970s.

He first came to Cape Clear in 1973 during a camping trip with his then-wife. They came for a day trip but failed to take note of the boat timetables and got stranded for three days. It was a very pleasant stranding, he recalls, and in 1979 they came back for good.

Island life has its challenges. Infrastructure, communications and housing must all be fought for. "It's Catch-22. There aren't enough people living on the island to make it worthwhile for the Government to put in services, and not enough services to make the island attractive for people to live on."

Ed runs his farm with the help of fellow adventurers who come on working holidays. When he advertises on the internet, he casually mentions that the accommodation is shared with himself and a German shepherd guide dog.

If they read carefully, new arrivals will have taken in this information by the time they land. If not, they will arrive on craggy Cape Clear to find the man who is to guide them through the twin arts of negotiating the rough landscape and successful goat rearing is himself guided by a dog, the hardy Zac.

"It's not a major issue for me, so it shouldn't be for them. But it does show that you should always read the small print," Ed grins.

Ed, who has also kept his previous guide dog, the now retired Casey, believes it is easier to live with blindness on an island than in a built-up urban environment. "I'm not going to be run over by a car because I can hear them coming. The exhausts are the first thing to go in the salty air!

"People ask about the cliffs and ask am I not afraid I'll topple over but that's what I have a dog for. The day I have a suicidal dog, I'm in trouble."

Ed Harper and Guide Dog Zac.

GERRY HAUGH
Student fundraising facilitator

SCHOOL days are full of tests but there are few as uniquely challenging as the legendary Belvedere College block pull.

Every summer, when exams are finished and uniforms are folded away, students from the Dublin boys' secondary school set off to cross Ireland from east to west on foot, pulling a float behind them and shaking buckets for coins on the way.

When the expedition was first undertaken in 1978, the boys made a giant replica of a typical Egyptian stone block to heave along on their float. The 'block pull', as it became known, was a success and a new school tradition was born.

Every year up to 50 students pack a rucksack, roll up a sleeping bag, and set off on the 10-day, 200-mile trek from Dublin to Galway, collecting jointly for Irish Guide Dogs for the Blind and Temple Street Children's Hospital as they go.

They take the long way around, shunning the by-passes and visiting as many towns as possible before settling down for the night in school halls or community centres.

If it sounds like a major production, then Gerry Haugh is the right man to direct the show. Gerry is an English teacher and head of drama at Belvedere and the block pull has been a regular feature of his summers since 1986.

"I just facilitate it – the students and parents are the ones who do the work," he says. "You just put up a notice about it and the room fills with volunteers."

The block pull is part of Belvedere's social justice programme. At Christmas, students take part in a 'sleep out' for the homeless. Others work in homes for street children in Calcutta and the school also has a very active branch of the St Vincent de Paul. But the Dublin to Galway trek has become a particularly important rite of passage for Belvedere students.

"They meet past pupils on the way who say they did it when they were in the school. It's a credit to the boys because it's fairly strenuous and we don't make it too comfortable for them. They get one night in a bed around the half-way point in Athlone but apart from that it's floors and sleeping bags. I have it easy because I get to drive the supplies."

The students know when they set out on the road that past pupil and guide dog owner, Philip O'Boyle, is cheering them on and camaraderie keeps their spirits up through blisters and downpours.

"We've raised over €1m on the block pull since it started; but, as well as that, it's a good exercise in getting to know each other. You have to talk to people when you're walking down the road with them for 25 miles. There's nobody shy by the end of the day."

ANN HIGGINS & DAVID LOHAN
Remembering Paul Higgins

THE memorial seat for Paul Higgins is positioned to greet the sun rising over Galway Bay in the morning and bid farewell to it as it retreats at night.

Paul loved this place where city meets sea and residents of the old Claddagh neighbourhood walk their dogs while children play and strollers take in the Atlantic air.

It was where he took his guide dog, Zac, to shake off the strains of the working day and where his wife, Ann, and good friend, David Lohan, remember him in rare moments of relaxation.

Paul died of a heart attack in 1998, just 44 years old and full of fervour, impatience and determination to better the lives of people who are blind.

"He used to say: 'Now's your chance, Ann – run,'" Ann recalls of the spirited teenager who stole her heart at the local youth club and then lost his sight to diabetes at the age of 17.

With the no-nonsense attitude that was typical of Paul, he prepared himself to lose his young sweetheart, too, but Ann never thought of leaving. "I was 18 when we got married. It sounds crazy now, but it was what we wanted."

There were hard times ahead. Paul received long cane training but the lack of independence frustrated him. When he finally got Zac, it turned both their lives around.

"I'll never forget the first day I saw Paul with Zac in town. I was going up by Brown Thomas and I just caught sight of them across the road, walking down the street. It was just unreal to see him being mobile and unstressed. It was a new lease of life."

From then on, Paul wanted to change the life of every blind person and he became a round-the-clock campaigner for Irish Guide Dogs for the Blind.

"He always said, if you lose your ability to walk, you get a wheelchair. He believed it was every blind person's entitlement to have a guide dog for mobility. It was a basic necessity, just like a wheelchair.

"Paul's death devastated me, our families and our friends. There was this massive void without him. But he wasn't someone to sit in a corner and get depressed. He would battle on and I suppose that rubbed off on me. I've come back to that way of feeling. I feel I am alive again. But it still pulls at the heart strings any time I see a guide dog."

David Lohan was one of those who felt Paul's loss deeply. David is an unashamedly old-fashioned pharmacist, mixing his own compounds and refusing to sell blusher and lipstick. "I didn't qualify to serve cosmetics," he grins. "I get my kicks out of helping people with how they are on the inside."

His passion for the welfare of the people of Galway earned him the title of Pharmacist of the Year in 2005 while in 2006 it brought him a Galway Person of the Year Award.

The 2006 awards panel were spoiled for choice in singing his praises for David is not only a caring community pharmacist but also a fundraiser for many charities and a strong supporter of the Galway Arts Festival and the Druid Theatre.

When he met Paul, he quickly added Irish Guide Dogs for the Blind to his list.
"If you want to give in a way that makes an immediate practical difference, then Guide Dogs are your man."

For all his practical ways, however, David admits to a bit of indulgence in erecting the memorial seat to Paul.

"I put the seat up in memory of Paul but really it was for me, because I was hurting. I could just hear Paul saying: 'That's very nice, Dave, but what about the Guide Dogs?' Only he mightn't have put it as politely as that. Paul was a straight-talker! So I said if I really want to do something for Paul, I'll do some of his work and raise money for a guide dog."

His fundraising efforts have since helped put other blind people on the path to getting a guide dog, just as Paul wanted to do. But David still likes to visit the seat which is hewn from local stone and carved in Braille.

"It's a place to sit and remember and to think ahead, too. Paul would be okay with that."

PJ HOGAN
Guide dog mobility instructor

PJ Hogan used to be a lab technician. The joke is that now he's a 'lab' technician.

Fine-tuning the skills of trainee labrador guide dogs is far more rewarding to him, however, than refining cider in a brewery or fertiliser in a chemical company.

PJ came to Irish Guide Dogs for the Blind in a roundabout way after getting itchy feet in a series of laboratory jobs. "My hobby at the time was scuba diving," he explains. "So I decided I would give up everything and move out to the Middle East."

He moved to Israel and got a job bringing divers to explore the Red Sea but when it was time to come home, he found it wasn't only the weather that was greyer – the economic climate was dismal too.

"It was the 1980s, the bleakest time here. I retrained but I still couldn't get a job. Then I saw an ad for an apprentice guide dog instructor. It sounded unusual, and I was attracted to the unusual."

The apprenticeship took three years but PJ knew long before the time was up that he had made the right choice.

"I realised very quickly the change that this could make to somebody's life. I'd had the freedom to make changes myself and I realised that blindness shouldn't hold people back – that if we just give them that extra prop, we give them the independence they need to do whatever they want."

One of PJ's key roles is that of matchmaker. "You have to match the dog to the person's needs. No two dogs are the same and no two people have the same requirements. You could have a person living in the country who rarely goes into town and a sociable dog who loves bustle is not going to be so happy there.

"People change as well, so a dog that they had before might not suit now. They could have been a working person living alone who is now married with a family, or a student living on campus who is now working and living on their own.

"We always have a list of people waiting for their first dog or a successor and there is an urgency to facilitate them, but the match must be right. Waiting can be frustrating – for us and the client."

PJ describes the job as a "life-long apprenticeship". "It's very much a heart and soul job as opposed to practical and functional. We are always coming into contact with people's lives and vice versa.

PJ with Goldendoodles Cash and Chad.

"But I wouldn't want to do anything else. It's like a different job every day so I'm not likely to get itchy feet again."

BRENDAN HOWLIN TD
Supporter

THERE are milestones in the development of every voluntary organisation – first premises, first client, first successful application for Government funds.

As Minister for Health in the early 1990s, Labour Party TD Brendan Howlin was able to facilitate that particular turning point in the financial life of Irish Guide Dogs for the Blind.

The country was still crawling out of recession but the Labour partners in the Labour- Fianna Fail coalition had insisted on creating a Department of Equality and Law Reform and established the principle that equality should underlie the work of all departments.

Irish Guide Dogs for the Blind promoted equality every day by ensuring blind and visually impaired people had equal opportunities for mobility and independence.

"It wasn't a time of great flushness of money in terms of supporting voluntary groups, so it was more a gesture of recognition than an attempt to underwrite any shortfall in funding," Deputy Howlin recalls of his grant to the organisation, "but I wanted to give a clear message that this was valuable work and that the State acknowledged it as such."

The State contribution increased over the years but the organisation still relies on voluntary donations for 80pc of its funding, a statistic Deputy Howlin says could do with improvement.

"We claim with great pride to be a republic, but the first litmus test of a real republic is that every citizen, regardless of age, gender, disability or however else society might try to categorise them, can vindicate full citizenship.

"For a person with a disability, that can mean very simple things like access to every public building and the ability to manoeuvre down every main street.

"It is to our great shame that we don't do enough in this area but people are forcing change because they are more assertive about their rights, which is a good thing. The 'God help them' view is gone and people are seen as needing practical support, not pity."

Deputy Howlin has always loved dogs and in 2006 he inaugurated the Howlin Cup, a perpetual trophy for the winner of the huge annual dog show run in his native Co Wexford by the Gorey branch of Irish Guide Dogs for the Blind.

Growing up in Wexford town, he had a cocker spaniel and later a fox terrier, and he would love to have another dog but the hectic schedule of a TD forbids it. He does, however, believe a few pets would be a welcome addition to Leinster House.

"A little pet therapy might be a good thing around the Dail," he muses. "I can think of one or two members it might calm down!"

DIANA & PETER JOHNSON
Grandchildren of Irish Guide Dogs for the Blind co-founder Mary Dunlop

TO the many people who came in contact with Mary Dunlop in the early years of Irish Guide Dogs for the Blind, she was Mrs D, a formidable campaigner, punctilious and perfectionist with a radar that could detect nonsense almost before it reached the tip of an unwise tongue.

To Diana and Peter, she was simply Nana, a woman of warmth and vitality who filled their childhoods with magic and left them with treasured memories.

Diana and Peter spent every Saturday of their schooldays with their Nana at her Currabinny home wedged between the woods and sea in her native Co Cork, where nature was all around.

"Nana had a huge affinity with animals and she was in her element at Currabinny," Diana says. "We saw her tame cats who were totally wild and she had robins eating out of her hand. The animals were as much a part of her family as we were."

There was no more important creature in Nana's life than Jan, her loyal German shepherd who took it upon himself to mind the grandchildren like they were his own pups.

"He was very strong and he would have protected us with his life but at agricultural shows Nana would have him jumping through hoops with a raw egg in his mouth in front of an audience," says Diana.

"Afterwards she would break the egg into a bowl and allow him to eat it to prove to the crowd that it wasn't hard-boiled. There was this great strength and gentleness at the same time – like Nana herself."

Mrs D was certainly a strong character. She was already in her sixties when she took on the challenge of setting up a guide dogs organisation in Ireland and she fought bureaucratic battles and financial barriers with vigour.

But she had also known sorrows that gave her a keen understanding of people's vulnerability and gentleness and compassion to match her resilience.

Her mother had died when she was born and during the war, she lost her own baby twins within weeks of their birth. In 1967, her beloved husband, Andrew, also died in a plane crash over the Pyrenees. It was a relative of Andrew's, much-loved Uncle Robbie, who inspired Mrs D to fundraise and establish links with Guide Dogs in Britain which would eventually lead to her founding an independent organisation Ireland.

Uncle Robbie was blind and it bothered her how restricted he was. Mrs D knew guide dogs equalled freedom and she reasoned that by showing off Jan's incredible obedience skills and dexterity at shows, she could demonstrate how highly trained a dog could become and convince people to support the cause.

She and Jan developed very public personas as a result of their non-stop rounds of the agricultural and horse show circuit but Diana says her Nana was an intensely private, modest person.

"She dreaded standing up and talking in front of people. People find that hard to imagine because they were used to seeing her in front of crowds. She was honoured with a People of the Year award in 1981 which she felt quite uncomfortable about. She always said it wasn't a personal award, it was an association award."

Peter recalls similar embarrassment for her when she was a guest on the Late Late Show in 1969. "It was the most exciting thing ever in our lives because as children we were allowed sit up and watch it but she was very reluctant to go on at all.

"We all laughed afterwards because she got a lovely letter from Gay Byrne thanking her for taking part when it was obvious to us watching the show that he was terrified of Jan!"

Mrs D died just before Christmas 2003. She was 91 and had spent her final hours talking about all that was dear to her, including her beloved organisation.

"We have got a lot of very, very happy memories," Diana says. "Lots of very proud memories of a wonderful grandmother which of course in her modesty she would say we should not have. I'd have to say sorry, Nana, but we are proud, very proud."

Zoe, Peter, Diana and Rusty.

Mary Dunlop,
Irish Guide Dogs for the Blind
Co-Founder
1912-2003

FRANCES JONES
Board member

RUSTY was Frances Jones's first love.

A mongrel with a bit of labrador and a lot of mischief in him, she bought him from the dogs' home for seven and sixpence out of her birthday money when she was 12 years old.

Her mother took one look at the tatty hound with the mangy coat, another look at her only child leading him by an old bit of string and a hopeful grin, took a deep breath, and gave her blessing to the unpromising partnership. It was the beginning of a love affair with dogs that was to shape the rest of Frances's life.

She enrolled Rusty's unruly successor, Sandy, in the obedience classes run by Irish Guide Dogs for the Blind co-founder, Mary Dunlop. Sandy learned to sit and stay - and Frances learned there was no such thing as sitting still where the campaign to develop Guide Dogs in Ireland was concerned.

She joined Mrs Dunlop and her German shepherd, Jan, on the rounds of agricultural shows where they gave obedience displays and Jan performed tricks. Unlike Jan, Sandy never got the hang of jumping through hoops but was a big hit padding around the audiences with a collection box on her back.

"The children loved this. You'd hear, 'Mammy, mammy, I want to give money to the doggy.' It was emotional blackmail really but it worked!"

In the early days of the organisation, there were no paid staff and Frances used every free day from her job as receptionist with Cork County Council to help fundraise and organise.

An orange yellow Volkswagen van holds special memories for her from that time. Once, while attending a meeting in Dublin, Frances, Mary Dunlop, Sandy, Jan and another labrador all slept in the van in the Phoenix Park to save on bed and breakfast bills.

Next morning, they smoothed their hair, shook the creases out of their clothes, slipped into the nearest hotel and boldly made use of the washroom facilities. Nowadays, the board does not encourage sleepovers in public parks and there are paid staff members – progress that makes Frances proud.

"In the early days we knew every single guide dog owner and the name of every dog. Then it dawned on me one day that I didn't know half the guide dogs and I raged about it, saying how impersonal it all was.

"But then I realised this was a good thing – it was a measure of our success. There should be too many guide dog owners for me to know individually. That means we're achieving exactly what we set out to do."

Frances Jones with goddaughter Jane Daly and Mr. Darcy.

NICKY KEALY
Guide dog owner

NICKY Kealy jokes that he should be included in tourist brochures because a sign erected on the pavement close to his Carlow town home makes him sound like a local attraction.

'Caution – Blind Person Crossing', it warns passing motorists. "Fifteen thousand vehicles pass that road every day," says Nicky. "I often wonder how many drivers think, 'Ooh, I wonder if I wait a while will I see the blind person crossing?'"

If he didn't crack jokes about it, he'd probably crack up over it. The 25-year-old has waged a lengthy war with town officials to get a proper pedestrian crossing installed but he reckons he's more likely to encounter little green men from Mars than a green man on a traffic light pole.

Nicky, a civil servant in the Department of Finance, lives in the town centre but must cross the busy N9 Dublin-Waterford route to get to the railway station so he can catch the train to work in Dublin each day.

Before the 'Caution' sign went up, his mother had to wake early every morning and travel from the family home on the edge of town to Nicky's house to drive him the three-minute journey to the train station.

"It kind of defeated the purpose of moving out of home in the first place. I didn't want to be in my twenties and still relying on my mother to get me out of the house in the morning!

"The sign is better than nothing but it's not good enough. Towns are meant to be for people to live in – not just for cars to drive through."

At least one aspect of Nicky's daily commute runs smoothly: his guide dog Ralph.
The pair negotiate the packed city streets with ease although bicycle couriers zig-zagging at speed along the footpaths have given them some hairy moments. "It's a FOOTpath!" Nicky says in bewilderment. "Even I can see that and I'm blind."

Lunch time brings a chance to walk off the stresses and Nicky and Ralph are chuffed to call Stephen's Green their garden as it is just minutes from the office. Fridays give them a break from the city as Nicky works from home then, proof-reading Braille translations of school and college text books for the National Braille Production Centre.

Since his battle with the local authorities over the road crossing, Nicky has found himself in demand as a spokesperson for the blind and other people with disabilities. He believes his time spent away from home as a child attending schools for the blind made him strong enough not to shy away from a fight.

"I don't have happy memories from that time. In fact I couldn't wait to get home at weekends. But it made me more assertive and better able to take care of myself so I'm confident enough to say what has to be said."

But while he has no problem speaking out, he would much rather be using his voice for other purposes. A seasoned musician who plays the keyboards and uileann pipes, Nicky is also a gifted singer who has recorded an album and works during his holidays for a United States cruise company, playing to passengers in the evening cabarets after a day soaking up the Caribbean sun.

"It's a tough job but someone has to do it!" he says. "I would love to make a full-time living out of music but that's the dream and in the meantime I have to make a wage while commuting like everyone else.

"That's why I get so annoyed about the accessibility of roads and paths. I've bought my own house and am doing everything I can to be independent. How crazy would it be that I'd have to ask the State to house me because I couldn't get across the road to get to work and pay the mortgage on my own home?

"People should not have to get militant to get basic entitlements. I'd prefer to be singing than shouting but I'll do whatever it takes."

ROY KEANE
Supporter

CROWDS and Roy Keane were made for each other. He draws them. They love him. Whether as footballer, manager, or figure of controversy – wherever Roy appears, a crowd follows.

It's what makes his support invaluable to Irish Guide Dogs for the Blind. Getting noticed can be difficult in a busy world but when Roy turns out for the organisation, attention is guaranteed.

But what Roy enjoys in return are the quiet, private moments away from the limelight when he gets to wander around the kennels in Cork, meet the dogs, chat to the staff, shake the hands of the owners.

"I met a gentleman from Bray at the kennels and he said, 'The dog got me here today'. He'd gone from Bray to Dublin on the DART, across town to the train, come to Cork and over to the centre, just himself and the dog – brilliant!" That's the buzz for Roy. No crowds required.

Roy was still at Manchester United and on the Republic of Ireland international squad when Irish Guide Dogs for the Blind approached him. As an organisation with its origins in his native Cork, and one that worked with dogs as well as people, it instantly drew his interest and he cautiously agreed to meet.

"Over the years since I came to England, I've been asked to get involved in different stuff," he explains, "but I always resisted committing myself to any one charity because I didn't think I had the time. If I commit to something, it would have to be 100 percent."

The meeting went well and Roy was sold. He jokes that he must have been caught in a weak moment. "Or maybe we'd won that week... yeah, I think that must have been it. Either way, I think I disappointed them – they thought I'd be a challenge."

Growing up in Mayfield in north Cork, the Keane children always had dogs in the family and Roy's own golden retriever, Triggs, is probably the best-known dog in soccer.

"There is a special quality to her. She is very placid and she's great with the kids," he says of the five young Keanes who keep Roy and his wife, Theresa, busy at home. "It's good for them too. It gives them something to care for....although they might train her to be a bit more disciplined instead of spoiling her!"

But while having a soft spot for dogs helped, Roy admits he had a lot to learn when it came to his adopted charity and the clients it serves.

"I didn't really appreciate what the dogs give to people – the independence which the rest of us take for granted. Being involved has opened my eyes. I received a letter from a lady thanking me for what I did. She told me that the dog gave her her life. She can go to the shops, to the post office, go on a train, on holidays. I am learning that this is what it's all about – dogs giving people their life."

Letters like that embarrass Roy a little. "The stuff I do is the tip of the iceberg," he insists. "The puppy walkers, the breeders, all the volunteers – they are the people who should be applauded."

Yet each year when Roy launches Shades Week, the national annual fundraising campaign, and when he turns out for other special events to raise awareness, all the cameras and microphones focus on him.

"That's okay," he says of the inevitable media clamour for photographs and comments on the latest footballing drama. "I'll do the interviews and stand for the photographs. If I'm going to be a face for Guide Dogs, I think half measures are not enough."

For him, the organisation works on the same motto. "They're moving forward all the time, trying different projects. The assistance dogs programme for autistic kids in fantastic. If you don't change, you get a bit stale.

"I'm grateful to be involved. I get a great buzz out of it. The benefit I get is when I go to the centre on a normal day and see people working away, giving 100 percent. These are the people who deserve the credit, not the Roy Keanes of the world. I do very little but hopefully it adds to the overall picture."

Roy Keane and Jagger.

KIERAN KENNEDY
Chief Executive, Irish Progressive Association for Autism

AUTISM has baffled doctors, bewildered teachers, and broken families.

To suggest that a dog could help where medicine, science, and love failed seems too simplistic to believe.

But a unique project has shown that there's something about canine companionship that helps autistic children to trust, connect, and communicate to an extent despairing parents had given up thinking was possible.

The dogs used in the joint venture by Irish Guide Dogs for the Blind and the Irish Progressive Association for Autism (IPAA) are specially trained 'assistance dogs' drawn from the Guide Dogs training programme.

Dogs fail to graduate as guide dogs for different reasons, but usually because of very minor imperfections. Once, there was no alternative but to find them good homes as pets; but since the discovery of their potential as assistance dogs, they are putting their skills and intellect to work in a new way.

The chief executive of the Cork-based IPAA, Kieran Kennedy, is himself the parent of an autistic child and is the first to admit he doesn't fully understand the dynamics between child and dog – he just knows that it works.

"When you meet the parents, you realise the difference a dog makes is not just to the child, but to the whole family. You can do things you never thought possible.

"In our case, we would be like eating machines. We eat a meal in five minutes flat. You can not relax. I meet parents now who tell me they can actually chew their food because their child is calm with the dog."

Some children are 'runners' who might take off at any given moment so parents can never let go of them; but with an assistance dog, the child is linked to the dog's lead and the dog lies down and prevents the child running away. Remarkably, children who can panic at any attempt at physical restraint don't seem to mind a dog acting as anchor.

"For some reason they seem to be able to bond with the dog. Autistic children lack empathy with other people, but the dog responds to what they do without challenging it or getting upset by it.

"The child seems to gain confidence from that and accepts the dog into their environment. It's not a threat and the child does not have to make sense of it."

The idea of assistance dogs for autistic children was pioneered in Canada and is still a relatively new idea in Ireland, but Kieran is thrilled with the results so far.

"We're seeing children transformed in months and even weeks. They're hugging the dog and then they start to do it with their parents. Imagine what it means to a parent who has never had a hug from their child before."

Kieran and Rocky.

KEVIN KENNEDY
Chairman, New York branch

IF proof was needed that a sense of community extends beyond geography, it can be found in a group of people who live in the United States but have Ireland residing in their hearts.

In New York city, from an apartment on the Upper East Side, the most far-flung branch of Irish Guide Dogs for the Blind is run. At its helm is Galway man Kevin Kennedy, who takes pride and pleasure out of bringing the city's Irish community together in support of the organisation.

Each fall, a familiar notice appears in the 'Irish Voice' newspaper, but the regulars need no reminder. The October fundraising dance is on in Rory Dolan's bar upstate in Yonkers and they'll be there, dancing to the Martin Melody Band and remembering similar nights 3,000 miles away on the other side of the Atlantic.

James Grogan from Tipperary is one of the first through the door followed by Olive and John Keegan from Longford, Kathleen Bramhall from Tipperary, Mae O'Driscoll from Cork, William Reynolds from Leitrim, Joe Flannery from Mayo, Kathleen Meehan from Cavan and the Sligo quartet of Martin Brett, Ray Conlon, Pat McGettrick and James Normanly.

Other friends and supporters include Sligo man, William Burke, President of the Country Bank; Dennis P Casey, President of the Galway Association; Sheila Grogan Barry; Sean McGovern from Donegal; and Clare man Danny Maloney of Liffey Van Lines Inc.

If word of mouth doesn't spread news of the gathering far enough, Mayo man Adrian Flannelly, presenter on WVNJ Radio, will get the message out with the help of CNN soccer analyst, Tommy Smyth from Louth, and his wife, Cork woman Treasa Goodwin, who co-host the Ireland Call programme on WVOX Radio. And when everyone is under the one roof, 'Irish Voice' photographer Nula Purcell is sure to be there with her camera.

The same crowd gathers when the branch sets up its stall at the Great Irish Fair in Coney Island each September, and they all meet again when Patrick McGowan and Shay Furlong of McGowan Builders run their annual fundraising golf outing for the organisation.

All these people owe their unity of purpose to the late Paul Higgins, a guide dog owner and tireless campaigner from Galway who delivered an impromptu address to a GAA function in New York one night on a visit to the city and left an inspired audience behind.

Kevin, a building superintendent in Manhattan, never imagined he would have such a strong community gathered around him when he first set foot in New York on a grey New Year's Day 1961.

"I landed at Idlewild Airport, before it was renamed after John F Kennedy, and there was six feet of snow on the ground. I stood looking around me and a man asked me what I was looking for. I said a plane to take me home. I still call Galway home but there's a bit of New York in me too. I'm glad I gave the place a chance!"

Kevin Kennedy

Back Row:
Ray Conlon, John Keegan, Pat McGettrick, Pat McGowan

Middle Row:
Bill Burke, Joe Flannery, Willie Reynolds, Jim Normanly, Shay Furlong

Front Row (Sitting):
Jim Grogan, Olive Keegan, Kathleen Bramhall, Kathleen Meehan, Eileen O'Hara, Martin Brett

BEN KENNY
Board member

GROWING up in 1950s Dublin, Ben Kenny didn't know which was worse – having to wear glasses or having the girls in the neighbourhood see him wear glasses.

Ben lived in Stoneybatter, then known as Cowtown because of the local cattle mart, and his regular chore was to collect buckets of manure for his parents' roses.

"I didn't mind that at all. I'd be going up the street with a bucket of cow dung spilling down my legs and that was fine … but, oh no, I wouldn't let the girls see me with glasses," he laughs.

Ben still wears glasses but his worst fears were never confirmed. He married Annette, a girl from up the road who really didn't mind that her beau came with frames attached.

The self-conscious boy of his youth was left even further behind when Ben joined An Post and worked his way up to a senior position in human resources where having the confidence to deal with people and their insecurities and idiosyncrasies was crucial.

"In HR, you are the peace-broker, the match-maker, the recruiter – everything that is required in keeping a large body of people working well together. It was always interesting."

It was while in An Post that Ben became acquainted with Irish Guide Dogs for the Blind. The organisation had submitted a request for an anniversary stamp and its chairman, Charlie Daly, thought it no harm to canvass Ben as Charlie's wife, Anne, had once worked alongside him.

Ben had no control over stamp design but he offered to help any other way he could. "I told Charlie I was getting three copies of 'Guidelines', the organisation's magazine, in the post and, while that was good for my employer, it showed up inefficiencies in his own operation. I offered a day's consultancy pro bono and he said, how about Thursday?"

The readiness of the organisation to listen to outside opinions and expert advice impressed Ben and that one day has so far stretched to a five-year involvement that continues to grow deeper.

After 32 years, he left An Post and now works his own hours as a HR consultant, which leaves him more time for Irish Guide Dogs for the Blind. His expertise is useful as he is determined to put all volunteers to good use and ensure people he calls the invisible hand in the organisation – background supporters like Annette – know they are valued.

But he also wants to create a little extra business for his old employers by creating a brand new address. "Our next target is a Guide Dogs centre in Dublin. I won't rest until we have that. I'll be thrilled when I see the first letters delivered there."

Ben and Annette Kenny

BERNADETTE KENNY
Guide dog owner

DO guide dogs eat your shoes? Bernadette Kenny has to be prepared for all sorts of questions when she goes to schools to talk to children about blindness.

But she isn't complaining. It's not so long ago that she feared she would never go out in public by herself, never mind address an audience.

Bernadette was nine years old when she developed a brain tumour and lost most of her sight. Her schooling was badly disrupted by her illness so now she's only too happy to help with the education of other youngsters.

"I was the youngest of a family of five when I got sick and I was very protected. I needed that protection but then as I got older I couldn't cope without it. I panicked if I was on my own and I just froze.

"People ask me how I got around before I got a dog. Well I used not to get around. I was under mammy's wing the whole time. If I ever did have to go anywhere myself, I used to get a taxi door to door."

Through inactivity, Bernadette gained weight which only made her less inclined to get out and about. She received long cane training in her early twenties but she still didn't have the confidence to walk alone.

By the time she was eventually persuaded to go to Irish Guide Dogs for the Blind for a dog, she weighed 22 stone and was miserable.

"We had to go to Mr Big, the outsize shop, to get raingear to fit me. I thought, 'I'll never survive the training.' That was probably my lowest point.

"Then I was introduced to Pete and we had to start walking together. I couldn't believe I was mobile. I was out one day after a few weeks in Cork and my waterproof trousers fell down because they were too big for me. I just laughed and laughed."

Pete, Bernadette's devoted golden retriever, now lives with her in their own flat. "It's only four doors down from my parents but

for me, that's another world. My ambition is to move further away – it'd be good for me and it'd make me stop calling in to mammy for meals. I haven't broken that habit yet!"

Since getting Pete, Bernadette has become chairperson of her local Irish Guide Dogs for the Blind branch in Walkinstown, Dublin, and has completed a fundraising cycle in Florida and the women's mini-marathon in Dublin.

She is also the honorary Lord Mayor of her neighbourhood of Greenhills, a title bestowed on her for her fundraising efforts for the local community centre.

"Mam started what we called 'The Benevolent' – a fund to look after women who were widowed in the locality, to make sure they could pay their bills and didn't lose their homes. That taught me about helping others. If I can give to just one other person what I've got, it'd make a difference.

"Since I got Pete I've lost weight, I've moved out of home, I've done the mini-marathon, I've flown in a plane – there's loads of things I never thought I've ever do. And I'm making plans. I want to do computer studies. I'm so independent now I don't know myself.

"Most of my life was just being at home under mammy's wing. I love my mam but I don't want to go back to that. I only want to move forward."

As well as talking to schoolchildren, Bernadette has made presentations to groups as diverse as ladies' clubs and a gathering of 68 leather-clad bikers

So, do guide dogs eat your shoes? "Of course not. Well, maybe the odd one. When they're not working, they're just dogs, you know, and they do dog things. Even when they are working, they still have their own personalities.

"Pete hates shopping. You get him into a shop and if you pass near the door at all while you're getting things, he just goes for it. I don't mind, though. I think it's gas that I, who wouldn't go anywhere, am the one encouraging him to come shopping."

Bernadette
and Guide Dog
Pete.

HAM LAMBERT
Former board member

OF all the treatments and techniques Ham Lambert came across in his long career as a veterinary surgeon, there were two he returned to time and again: respect and instinct.

Noel Hamilton Lambert followed his father and grandfather into veterinary medicine, graduating from veterinary college in 1931 when attitudes to animals were quite different from now.

Horses were for transport and pulling power, making them essential to industry and deserving of reasonable levels of care; cattle were for food and came next in the pecking order; but pet cats and dogs were an indulgence and only a fool or a rich man would call a vet instead of a rifle for them when they were sick.

But Ham couldn't help himself – he liked dogs and cats. More than that, he respected them. After learning the ropes in his father's draught horse practice and developing his own cattle practice in the heart of his native Dublin, he turned his attentions to pets.

As it was a much-neglected area, he had a lot to learn; Ham eagerly accepted advice from vets abroad who had more experience than he. Never afraid to try something new, he marvelled at the advances in technology and medicine that today's vets have at their disposal.

For him, the one tool that never became outdated, however, was instinct. Ham learned to trust what he saw, smelt, and felt in an animal and, to him, the greatest diagnostic devices a vet could have were his own senses.

He was met by scepticism when he began using osteopathy on lame animals but he happily demonstrated that, by the touch of his own fingers, he could find a problem and manipulate the most minutely disjointed bone back into place: no X-rays, no surgery, and no expensive bills.

He also raised eyebrows for his faith in the healing powers of Vitamin E, but he never let negative reactions bother him. Curing an animal was reward enough.

His refusal to be tied by convention made him invaluable to Dublin Zoo. Little was known about treating many of the exotic species residing there but Ham was not afraid to try and he gave his services free of charge for many years.

He felt the same about Irish Guide Dogs for the Blind. He was serving as veterinary inspector for the long-running St Patrick's Day Dog Show in Dublin when he met the organisation's co-founder, Mary Dunlop, and came away determined to set up a branch in the capital.

Over the years he was fundraiser for the organisation, physician to the dogs, and friend to the owners … and he never took a penny in return.

It was never all work and no play, however, for Ham had an outstanding record as a sportsman, earning caps for Ireland in both rugby and cricket. When a knee injury put paid to his rugby career, he switched to refereeing and was involved in some of the biggest international matches of the 1940s and 1950s.

He was still a referee assessor in his nineties and held a golf handicap that would delight men half his age. He found it impossible to pass a television channel showing a tennis match, a game of snooker, or just about any other sport in existence.

His late wife, Jean, never had to worry about him getting under her feet when they retired to Enniskerry, Co Wicklow, and their children, Bruce, a doctor; Jeanette, a podiatrist; and Mark, an actor and theatre director, were in awe of their father's energy, which never seemed to dwindle with age.

As Irish Guide Dogs for the Blind was marking its 30th year, Ham was celebrating his 96th. Sadly, he passed away as this book was being prepared.

He is remembered by the greyhound industry as one of most gifted vets ever to place a hand on a valuable competition dog. But although he loved the fine-bred pedigrees of the race track, the dogs that had the run of the Lambert household were usually mongrels, strays, and cast-outs.

One in particular, a nondescript pup called Fred found abandoned on the roadside in Ham's retirement years, became the living embodiment of his belief that dogs have an intelligence, loyalty, and capacity for unconditional love that deserves in return responsible ownership, warmth of heart, and, above all, respect.

Ham scores a try for
Leinster v Munster in 1934.

TOM LANGAN
Guide dog owner and former board member

THE fields around Abbeyknockmoy struggled to feed the families who toiled there when Tom Langan was a boy but one thing that flourished in the rugged soils was a work ethic.

"I grew up in a family where being idle was not acceptable," says Tom. "Everybody had a contribution to make, no matter how big or small, and an extra pair of hands was always useful."

Those experiences from his East Galway childhood would both drive and frustrate Tom in the years ahead as he fought to find his own place in the labour force against all the obstacles that blindness threw at him.

Tom was born with retinitis pigmentosa, although it did not become obvious until he began school. "That was the early 1950s and there wasn't much in the way of services or education around," Tom recalls. "Blindness was seen as quite a debilitating disability and it would have brought a lot of fear and apprehension to my mother."

The headmaster tried to keep her fears at bay, encouraging Tom to participate in all the lessons by listening. But, by the age of 12, it was clear he needed specialist training and he was sent to St Joseph's boarding school for blind boys in Dublin.

Tom is diplomatic in recalling his time there: "It was very much of the 1960s. We were just children, so we took everything as normal."

When he left St Joseph's at 17, Tom knew his employment options were limited but, as luck would have it, there was a position going as an apprentice piano tuner at the famous Rippon factory in Shannon.

"It was the making of me. I knew nothing about the world, but my time there changed from a naive boarding school boy to a working man."

Tom was there less than four years when the factory closed and he returned home to the farm, back to gathering turf and hay. But word of mouth led him to hear about a telephonist in the county council who was blind. Tom made his acquaintance, learned the ropes from him, and got himself a job with the Western Health Board.

"Employment is so important," he says. "It's the most important thing after education and mobility. It gives you financial independence, it gives you a social life and it gives you an opportunity to develop your skills."

But it also gave Tom an aversion to charity so, while he was keen to get a guide dog, he was reluctant to put himself in the hands of Irish Guide Dogs for the Blind.

"I was afraid they would see me as someone who had to be taken care of. I didn't want to feel like a charity case. Those of us who had found work and independence had a resistance to being taken care of."

A meeting with the organisation's founders, Jim Dennehy and Mary Dunlop, swiftly dispelled Tom's fears. "They didn't want to take care of me – they wanted to give me a dog so I could take care of myself."

Tom got his first dog in 1978 and currently has Trigger, his fifth. Though he only met his wife, Mary, in his forties, he jokes that he already had plenty of experience with marriage because the partnership he developed with each dog was like being wed.

He became a key member of Irish Guide Dogs for the Blind, helping the organisation develop its training programme and setting up the Galway branch. He also got involved in labour rights and remains a passionate trade unionist.

"Unions are needed more than ever today. When I started work, a job was a job for life but now it's all temporary contracts and, for people with disabilities on a succession of contracts, it's very hard to get a mortgage."

"The unions have been a great platform for creating opportunities for people with social disadvantage. They've always been open to people with disability and ensuring that you get a leg up. That's the philosophy of Guide Dogs – give them a leg up and let them off."

Tom with Guide Dog Trigger.

DERRY LAWLOR
Guide dog owner

EVERY city has its mean streets but it isn't only the human inhabitants who suffer the cruelty.

When Derry Lawlor was mugged while walking in his native Dublin with his first guide dog, Jessie, the fear, shock and anger he felt took time to fade. But for Jessie, the ordeal was one even time wouldn't heal.

"Jessie became aggressive towards strangers. It was understandable, given what happened, but if you're going to be out and about you're going to meet a lot of strangers and in a city like Dublin you don't have a path all to yourself. So Jessie had to be retired. I was heartbroken.

"People asked did the mugger take anything. Only the invaluable things – my confidence and my mobility. I didn't want to go out. Then when I did, I went everywhere in a taxi. But eventually I got back to myself and decided enough of this, I want back out into the world."

Derry was teamed up with a new dog, Barry, and had nine years of successful partnership but there was to be more heartache ahead. When Barry retired, his successor was Charlie who endured a Halloween from hell one year with bangers and rockets exploding all around the house.

"We got medication from the vet to calm him but the damage was done. He became fretful of sudden noises and that wasn't much good for a dog in the city so we had to go through another early retirement. It was terrible."

Then along came Lottie. "She's such a city girl. She loves exploring – you have to stop her if she passes a new laneway or she'll be down it just to check it out. She nearly gets stood on in the bus on the way to work every morning and she doesn't mind. She's been on the Tube in London without a bother. I'd still be anxious around Halloween. One bad fright can ruin a dog. But she's fine with noise and hassle, so I don't worry generally.

"The matching programme that Irish Guide Dogs for the Blind have is improving all the time. They've got very good at pairing off people with the best dog for where you live and what you do. They should go into the matchmaking business for humans – no more lonely hearts!"

Derry had to rely on Cupid to look after his own matchmaking but he's happy to report that the arrow hit it target. He lost his sight to a pituitary tumour at the age of 10 and it was while training in telephony in Sligo some years later that he met fellow trainee, Martha. They married in 1991.

Derry and Martha take the same route to work each morning, battling the commuter crush on the number 19 bus into the city centre. Martha works as a telephonist at the Department of Enterprise, Trade and Employment while Derry's office is across the road in the Department of Agriculture and Food.

As a senior computer programmer, his duties include administering the staff rosters, payslips and flexitime arrangements. "So they have to be nice to me," he grins. "It wouldn't do to upset the man with the payslips."

He and Martha share a love of travel, are apprentice wine buffs and are gadget-mad.
They both surf the web and email on a speaking computer and Martha has enough sight to read with the help of a magnification scanner.

Derry has created a speaking filing system for his DVD collection and has a global positioning satellite device that works as a speaking map to tell the user what street they are on, what buildings of note they are passing and what lies ahead.

"We usually go every year to the Sight Village exhibition in Birmingham to see what's new. They've got computers that let you do anything you want. About the only thing they can't let you do is drive or fly, but you never know!

"They'll probably come up with computerised dogs too, so you don't have to worry about muggers and bangers, but I don't think I'd be swapping Lottie for one. A computer can't lick your hand to tell you everything's all right."

Martha, Derry and Guide Dog Lottie.

BILL & KEVIN LYNCH
Supporters

FATHERS usually try to set an example for their sons to follow but with Bill and Kevin Lynch it was more a case of like son, like father.

Like all schoolboys, 13-year-old Kevin had a favourite haunt: every chance he got, he was off down the road to Irish Guide Dogs for the Blind national headquarters and training centre a few minutes from his Cork city home.

"He was always down there, looking in at the dogs and talking to the staff," Bill explains. "The next thing he tells me he wants to raise money for the organisation and I told him to go ahead and come up with a plan, and suddenly he's organising a collection at his school."

The next year Kevin organised a cake sale, and the year after, a sponsored run. All this time, he was still in primary school, St Joseph's National School, where principal Damien Keane and teacher Ruth Kelleher proved strong allies.

"The school is very supportive of the pupils and not just in a purely academic way," says Bill. "Mind you, Kevin is a hard man to say no to! If he doesn't get a straight answer, he keeps going until he does."

Bill discovered the persuasive powers of his elder son himself when Kevin put a proposition to him. Bill and his brother, Leonard, have the franchise for O'Brien's Sandwich Bars in Cork city and Kevin decided their counters would be the ideal place to position collection boxes.

"We were already doing a lot of work with the Christina Noble Children's Foundation but Kevin approached me and said he needed to do something big if he was going to surpass the total he raised the previous year. He was able to convince me so we adopted Guide Dogs too."

Kevin's work has had an effect on all the Lynches. Brother, Robert (11) and sister Clodagh (8) were thrilled when the family was allowed give a home to Kane, a lovable labrador who didn't graduate from guide dog training school; and mum, Noreen, who was never mad about dogs, has been well and truly converted.

But Kevin dismisses the idea that his efforts amount to hard work. "I enjoy it so it isn't like work. I just loved the dogs and wanted to do something for them."

Kevin moved to secondary school in 2006, to Presentation Brothers College, but was planning to bring his fundraising campaign with him.

"I've no doubt his new principal will be hearing from him before long!" says Bill. "We're very proud of him. People always say children are the future but Kevin's doing something now that makes a difference to the present. That makes him very special."

Bill, Kevin and Kane.

PEG LYONS
Guide dog owner

IF Peg Lyons has one piece of advice to offer, it is to be bold.

Peg knew nothing about England when she made up her mind to go there in January 1949 after reading a notice in a Braille magazine about a pilot training scheme for shorthand typists run by the National Institute for the Blind in London.

"I didn't even know what shorthand typing was. I just said - that's for me," she laughs. "Somehow I convinced the Dun Laoghaire Borough to give me a scholarship and away I went. It was utterly stupid, really."

It might have been stupid if she didn't have the determination to match her boldness, but Peg had both in bucket loads. She has been told that she lost her sight to meningitis at one year of age, though she has no memory of ever having sight.

What she does remember is a protective mother who couldn't bear to send her vulnerable little daughter away to the school for the blind so that Peg didn't even begin to learn Braille until she was a teenager.

She remembers long, lonely years at home with nothing to do as her teens gave way to her twenties. It was then she decided she would have to take a bold step forward.

"I knew that, no matter how I did it, I was going to change my life. I didn't know how. I had no money. I had no experience. But then I read the notice in the magazine. It's kind of a miracle how things changed."

Peg spent a year in England, gaining skills to work in an office environment and meeting her future husband, Pat, who had also travelled from Ireland and was training in telephony.

On their return, Peg worked in various jobs before getting a post in the old Department of External Affairs, now Foreign Affairs. But to her despair, she had to leave when she married Pat, as the law at the time forbade married women to work in the civil service. After all the obstacles she had overcome to secure her independence, she couldn't believe she was to be beaten by bureaucracy.

"We accepted too many things at that time. People of my generation didn't challenge things enough. Whoever made those laws, they owe us so much, they could never repay us."

Despite having to give up her hard-won job, Peg remained determined to live a full life. She applied for and received her first guide dog from England in 1961 and before long she had a baby son and daughter to keep her busy too.

"I didn't know much about dogs or children, so it was pretty difficult. Pat and I got very little help as parents and we had very little money. But, however difficult things were, I always found the dogs helped me. They were a practical help in getting around of course but also, when I was with the children all day, to be able to get out by myself in the evening was marvellous. The dog had to be walked so there was never an argument about it."

Peg and Pat began to edit a magazine for the blind in their spare time so Peg found herself dusting off her old office skills and learning a few new ones when she took another bold step and acquired a personal computer.

Now widowed, Peg has recently gone back to her computer and is learning to use the internet as she is determined to keep in touch by email with her daughter and five grandchildren who live in Chicago.

Peg's guide dog, Huey, is her sixth and she has also kept Frieda, who was number five and is now retired. She loves their daily strolls to the shops or around her neighbourhood and says she will never be without a guide dog.

"When I did my training with Huey I had to put everything I knew into it because I'm not as fresh as I was; but older people like me should always be careful never to say I'm too old. They have to try. You don't know what you can achieve until you try. You must be bold."

Peg Lyons with Guide Dog Huey.

122

123

JIMMY MANGAN
Supporter

A MOMENT'S glory can yield a lifetime of memories and there was none more glorious or memorable for Jimmy Mangan than when he trained the winner of the Aintree Grand National.

Approaching Conna village close to Cork's border with Co Waterford, a large sign welcomes visitors and informs them they're in the home of Monty's Pass, Grand National hero of 2003.

Everyone in the village and many outside know everything about the racing feats of the horse who still occupies a special place in Mangan's yard and there is never a shortage of inquiries after him and requests for photographs with him.

Less well known, however, are his efforts for Irish Guide Dogs for the Blind. Before the Turf Club stopped charity races on safety grounds, Jimmy used to enter a horse in the annual fundraising gallop at Mallow.

He had already promised to put Monty into the 2003 event when they set out for Aintree, never imagining he would be coming home as Grand National winner. Jimmy's wife, Mary, took the place that jockey Barry Geraghty held at Aintree. "As if I'd let anyone else!" she says.

Monty won the race – his last ever win – and the crowd went into raptures. "It was incredible, really, the reception that Mary got," says Jimmy. "It was like being at Aintree all over again."

One of the questions Jimmy is most often asked is what makes a winning horse, and he replies that it's all about temperament.

"The training's important but as a trainer you have to work with the animal you have in front of you and the characteristics they're born with. Monty is very intelligent. He has everything you would look for – a great brain and he is cool, calm and collected to go with it.

"I imagine it's the same with guide dogs. The training they get is unbelievable but you need a good dog to start with – one with a cool head."

Jimmy has a young relative, eight-year-old Donal Ahern, who is visually impaired and, he is fascinated by the bond that has grown up between the boy and his dog, Abby, a former trainee guide dog who did not graduate.

"It's fantastic what even dogs who don't make the grade as guide dogs can do. What they're doing for children with autism is unbelievable. They have a way with children that maybe adults don't understand.

"It's the same with horses. It's hard to know the workings of their mind. The thing is to find the key and then use it. If the key to an autistic child is a dog, then so be it."

Jimmy, wife Mary with 2003 Aintree Grand National Winner Monty's Pass.

BRIAN MANNING
Guide dog owner

BRIAN Manning has a deal with his fellow motorbike enthusiasts in the Goldwing Club when they go on touring holidays – they find the locations and he provides the history.

"They're typical bikers – they just like the look of a place! But I love the history. On our last trip we rode down to Dubrovnik, the ancient walled city at the tip of Croatia, so we had beauty as well as history and everyone was happy."

Brian's fascination with the past led him take history with sociology as his degree course at University College Cork where he made history of his own just by being there. Born in Cork city with congenital glaucoma, he was not expected to achieve academically because it didn't seem possible that a blind boy could match the pace in a regular school.

But Brian had expectations and, with the encouragement of teachers, he left school with a Leaving Cert good enough to get into university. That was the only start of his battles.

UCC had no facilities for visually impaired students and doubted he would cope. Brian convinced the authorities otherwise and set in train a chain of events that transformed the college for every student with a disability who came after him.

A social worker he knew from the National Council for the Blind in Ireland had a friend in the college library who agreed to set up a voluntary reading pool for him. She recruited people to read chapters from Brian's textbooks on to hundreds of audio cassettes he bought and, with their help, he got through first year.

In his second year, the college authorities gave his librarian friend time off her regular duties to devote to the recording sessions. She went on to help set up the college's progressive Disability Support Service which now assists up to 400 students every year.

"I often said the organisation it took for me to be in college was the hard part rather than the academic aspect," Brian says. "That's changed for the better for students now."

The organising became easier when Brian got his first guide dog, Willow, but he didn't take the step lightly. "I didn't want a dog. I thought as long as I don't bump into things too much, no-one will know I can't see; whereas, if I get a dog it will be like a label. But once I got the dog and realised the freedom she gave me, I couldn't understand why I didn't have one before."

Brian's current job is all about giving freedom to blind and visually impaired people. He works in IT training and technical support for the National Council for the Blind and travels all over Cork and Kerry with current guide dog, Heidi, to meet clients.

"It's about independent living. Whether you're getting information about your local area, finding out your rights and entitlements, checking what's on in the theatre, reading newspapers, going shopping on-line or keeping in touch with others by email, you can use your computer as a tool of independent living. We teach people to use that tool.

"It's not so different from regular computer training except that if you are blind, instead of looking to learn, you are listening to learn."

One difference, however, is cost. Adapted computers and specialist software are expensive and grant aid is limited. "It's one of the downsides of my job. I go to people's homes and schools and I tell them of the excellent technology that's available and how it's going to make them more independent and then I have to tell them the cost. It's almost as if I dangle a carrot and then take it away again."

Still, Brian gets a huge kick out of developments in assistive technology, especially when he recalls his own early efforts in college.

"For my first sociology essay, I spent two nights manually typing eight pages and then gave them to my sister to retype so they would be neat. She went quiet when I handed them to her – the typewriter ribbon had broken and the pages were blank.

"I see the students now with their laptops and their MP3 books and it's great. I'm jealous, of course, but in a good way."

Brian and Guide Dog Heidi.

GEORGE MANSFIELD
Committee member

GEORGE Mansfield knows exactly what it's like for a company facing endless appeals for charitable donations.

In his job as a senior manager with AIB bank, he received almost daily requests for sponsorship from all kinds of good causes and had the difficult task of deciding which he could help and which would have to wait.

Since his retirement, his insider knowledge has been invaluable to Irish Guide Dogs for the Blind. Now George is the one approaching the corporate sector and convincing businesses to dip into their pockets.

"Big companies get inundated with requests, but if you make the case, and make it well, there is money available. Companies expect to be asked – they just want to be sure their money will be spent well. If you have a good cause, and you explain it properly, you will get good support."

Guide Dogs proved an irresistible organisation for George, who has long had a love of labradors. Some people populate their lawns with garden gnomes or Grecian goddesses but two tall labrador sculptures form the centrepiece of George's own oasis in Cork city.

He also confesses to having his all-time favourite labrador, Jock, buried in his own special plot among the flowerbeds, although he doesn't say that out loud when current pal, Ernie, is around.

Hurling, football, Manchester United and grandchildren make up the other delights of retirement for George.

"It took a little while to adjust," he admits of winding down from the hectic days of high finance. "I was 40 years with the bank. If you went to the bank the time I joined, it was like being in a monastery. It was a position for life and it was the entire focus of your life.

"Suddenly you have time for family and for things like Guide Dogs that you hardly knew existed because you were on a certain path and they just didn't cross it.

"Being involved in Guide Dogs is a great leveller. You start appreciating the simple things that you have taken for granted. It doesn't matter what status you have in life - if you lose your sight, you have to start again and learn again. It has opened my eyes in a big way.

"People can put off being involved in a charity if they think they're going to be asked to do everything but the way I see it, no one person should take it on themselves to be overburdened.

"Everyone gives a bit and you build a great big mountain of expertise. That's how businesses do it – that's how voluntary organisations can succeed too."

George with grandson Raymond, grand daughter Rachel and Ernie

MICHEÁL MARTIN
Minister for Enterprise, Trade and Employment

MINISTER Micheál Martin is uniquely placed in Cabinet to know the work of Irish Guide Dogs for the Blind. Born and bred in the organisation's home in Cork, he saw the pups being walked and trained on the city's streets, and as Lord Mayor in the early days of his political career, he became its patron and regular visitor.

As a newly qualified secondary school teacher, the minister had seen for himself how blindness did not have to be a barrier to success. The new recruit to St Kieran's College was quickly taken in charge by the late Pearse Leahy, without knowing that the respected schoolmaster was blind.

"He taught Leaving Cert honours classes through audio tapes but that was the only way you would have known. He never adverted to the fact that he was blind and he never allowed it to undermine his ambitions or achievements."

Some years later, Minister Martin was struck by the same characteristic in Jim Dennehy, President of Irish Guide Dogs for the Blind. "When you meet Jim and his wife, Pat, you see an independence there that you have to respect – not just independence in practical ways but in thought as well, and there is great vision – the kind blindness doesn't affect."

As Minister for Health, he helped make that vision a reality when he allocated substantial funding towards the new National Headquarters and Training Centre, which opened in 2001 on the site of the crumbling old farmhouse that previously housed the organisation.

"I was very happy to be able to help. The people in the organisation are infectious in the way they approach their tasks. There is a sense of celebration, notwithstanding the difficulties and challenges facing them, and that positive approach wins a lot of respect."

In more recent times, Minister Martin has watched with interest the developments in the assistance dog programme for autistic children.

"When I was Minister for Education in 1998, we set out the first teacher-pupil ratio for children with autism. It's hard to imagine that before then, these children weren't defined as having separate, specialist educational needs. This programme shows there are new hopes for autism."

Minister Martin is also keen to see the organisation follow through on ambitions to open a centre in Dublin to cater for the many clients on the eastern side of the country as well as the growing band of puppy walkers and other volunteers in the region.

"I think it would be a very positive development and it's something I would be anxious to support. I can see it happening. I get a sense from Guide Dogs that they are not standing still. They are constantly looking at ways to do things better rather than saying that's it, we'll rest on our laurels now. It's that positive approach again. It's hard not to be drawn to it."

ISABEL McDONOUGH
Branch secretary

LISTOWEL will always be known as a town of characters thanks to the plays of John B Keane, but Isabel McDonough also knows a few canine characters who would enliven any stage.

Her childhood family pets were scotch terriers called Bruce and Bonny who earned themselves a reputation as the town time-keepers.

Bruce and Bonny would wake the family each morning, wait to be let out, and set off walking through the streets. They would cross the busy square and on to the last house on the edge of town where Isabel's grandmother lived and a hearty breakfast awaited.

"I remember a man who lived down town greeting my parents one day and saying, 'You slept in this morning'. They were baffled and then he explained. 'The dogs were late passing the house.'"

Pups with personality still reside in Listowel, and Isabel and her fellow members of the local branch of Irish Guide Dogs for the Blind get to meet them once a year at the annual fundraising dog walk and show.

"Up to 100 dogs take part in the walk and there is a massive volume of noise. Most of this is generated by Scampi, my daughter's west highland terrier although there was competition this year from Daisy, a westy pup owned by my friend Paula, wife of our treasurer, Paul Murphy.

"Daisy was the smallest dog on show but in her excitement she somehow managed to shout down a great dane the size of a calf! Characters like that make the day."

The walk is organised by a dedicated crew of branch members, relatives and friends who all pitch in to give a hand. They operate on the theory that the committee that plays together, stays together, so they make sure to have fun.

"We do a churchgate collection every February which is a bit damp but productive so we enjoy it. Our regular branch meetings are conducted in a local pub. The business of the organisation is always fully dealt with but we don't neglect to consume a beverage or two while we're at it."

Isabel has recruited the support of her solicitor husband, Louis, in the branch's fundraising endeavours and he in turn has spread the word among his many friends and contacts in the legal profession who contribute generously.

The couple's three daughters, Emma, Sarah and Lisa, are also regularly, but willingly, conscripted to help out, as are a long list of family members that extends right down to Isabel's sister's two labradors.

"Even the dogs do their bit by coming out to fundraise with us. After Bruce and Bonny, they have a tradition of service to the town to live up to!"

JILL McELROY
Fundraiser

NEVER work with children and animals, the old rule advises, but Jill McElroy doesn't heed rules much.

She first got in touch with Irish Guide Dogs for the Blind through her involvement in bringing Chernobyl children on holiday to Tramore, Co Waterford. Most of the children who visit are not only orphans and suffering from radiation illness, but are also partially sighted or blind.

"One of the first things we do when they come over is get their eyes checked. There is virtually nothing for them at home. Up to the age of 16, or 18 if they are lucky, they are looked after but then they could disappear off the face of the earth. That's the harsh reality of living in a poor country."

The experience led Jill to Irish Guide Dogs for the Blind and she and a group of friends have taken on a leading role in reviving the Tramore-Waterford branch.

"I am the chairperson, secretary, treasurer and PRO - whatever needs doing at any given time. We don't have a strict committee structure because we find that we can sort things out over the phone or a cup of coffee rather than a formal meeting."

The group was boosted by the arrival of Lacey, a lovable labrador who accompanies Jill and her team on flag days along the packed summer strand of Tramore and at other strategic collection spots.

Lacey also visits schools on education trips. "She has had 200 children hanging out of her in a day and she thinks it's wonderful."

Like dog, like owner. Jill keeps up her work with the Chernobyl children, has joined the Tramore Special Olympics Club and is also involved in a new Motor Activities Club for children with severe disabilities.

They arrange fun activities that encourage movement, co-ordination and, like Guide Dogs, a can-do attitude.

"The first time I met some of the children I came away and cried. To see children utterly unable to do anything for themselves is heartbreaking. But then to see them try and succeed in simple tasks is also very heartening."

A mother of six grown children, Jill shares her home with Lacey, two cocker spaniels, a retriever, and a cat as well as, on occasions, her son's two boxers and his very vocal parrot.

The brazen bird mimics Jill calling the dogs and does a flawless imitation of a ringing phone. The dogs have learned not to be fooled by his cheeky commands but visitors regularly get caught out and start rummaging for imaginary phones.

"It just proves," says Jill, "sometimes animals really are smarter than humans."

Anne Kenneally with Guide Dog Puppy Marco,
Jill McElroy with Fundraising Dog Lacey and
Carmel Nairn with Guide Dog Puppy Orri.

MARGARET McGAHON
Fundraiser

ACTORS may deal in make-believe but one made an indelible difference to Margaret McGahon's life.

It was 1985 and Margaret was grieving following the death of the beloved grandmother who had reared her. It was also when 'Glenroe' was the most popular homegrown drama on television.

Margaret, herself a sheep farmer like the characters Dinny and Miley Byrne, was a firm fan. "I was feeling a bit down in myself and I heard Mick Lally, Miley as he was, on the radio publicising a sponsored dog walk for Irish Guide Dogs for the Blind. It perked me up and I got involved from there."

Every year since, Margaret has organised walks, carried out collections and kept the organisation's profile high in Co Louth, not least by walking in local St Patrick's Day parades dressed as St Patrick, accompanied by her golden retriever, Captain, and leading a pet sheep wearing a leprechaun hat.

"We get great fun out of it. Everyone loves to see Captain and the sheep loves the attention. She's more like a dog because she's always around the other pets."

The other pets include eight dogs, 13 cats, hens, ducks, geese, a turkey, a pony, more sheep and a goat. "Nothing gets killed, eaten, or sold," she laughs. "People say it's a zoo I should have, not a farm."

On the working part of the farm, however, there is plenty of labouring to be done. But although Margaret and her husband, Hugh, are both pensioners, they have no desire to leave the land.

"Once you're happy at it, why would you stop? We're not doing it to get rich. Once you have a bit to eat, a bed to lay in and a few bob to go to the shop, that's all you need.

"I'm tired of people saying I need this and I want that. If you have 40 rooms in the house, you can still only sleep in one. People laugh at me and say I'm back in the 18th century but I don't care."

Margaret's old-fashioned philosophy helped her prepare for what looked like certain disaster when the foot and mouth crisis in 2001 threatened their Castlebellingham farm.

"The river saved us. That's where the line was drawn. No-one could visit us for ages, not even the postman. But we were lucky. Neighbours and friends were destroyed. It was heart-breaking.

"But people are strong and they get on. You see that with Guide Dogs. It's a terrible knock if your whole life changes – whether you lose your sight or there's some other disaster – but people get up and get on. We're a strong breed."

Margaret with
Captain and Bell.

MARIE McGETTIGAN
Fundraiser

MARIE McGettigan knew nursing was supposed to be a vocation but secretly she saw it as more of a vacation.

She was having a dull time working in the local tax office in her native Donegal town when she latched on to nursing training in England as a pathway to adventure.

"I just wanted to go to England. Other girls were going and I thought there'd be a great buzz. To me it was about having a good time. But I surprised myself - I loved the nursing too."

She got the adventure as well when she returned to work in accident and emergency across the border in Derry. The Troubles had erupted, the streets were full of soldiers and whenever there was a riot, shooting or bombing, the hospital was at the centre of the action. "There was a buzz then, all right! We were certainly kept busy."

Marie later switched to a calmer but no less challenging type of nursing when she cared for elderly patients and young people with disabilities at the Royal Hospital in Dublin's Donnybrook.

She was an early advocate of pet therapy and used to bring her springer spaniel, Fritz, to work to mix with the patients. The idea attracted the interest of a television crew and the resulting broadcast brought an invitation from a local Irish

Guide Dogs for the Blind member to take part in a sponsored dog walk for the organisation. Marie and Fritz quickly became active members.

Marie loved the Royal and was shaken when a recurring back problem forced her into early retirement. "I thought, What am I going to do? How am I going to live?" she recalls.

Homing instinct brought her back to Donegal but the move didn't go smoothly. She bought out the old family home, renovated it from top to bottom, but then saw it burn down after an adjacent premises caught fire.

"I thought, I can do one of two things: I can sit down and cry or I can say luck is with me because no-one is hurt. I decided luck was me and I haven't looked back."

Since then, Marie has fulfilled a dream of running a small kennels and she spends all her free time on fundraising and awareness campaigns for Irish Guide Dogs for the Blind.

"I'm delighted how things worked out and I have to credit Guide Dogs. Anybody I ever met with a guide dog has been an inspiration to me, the way they accept life and the challenges it throws up. It makes me look at challenges as an adventure and, like I learned early on, a bit of adventure does you good."

Marie with Fundraising Dog Hudson

CAITRIONA McGROARY WALSH
Corporate social responsibility co-ordinator

IN the hotel business, going the extra mile for a guest can mean the difference between passing trade and a customer for life, but for Caitriona McGroary Walsh it even meant finding a partner for life.

The care Caitriona took to restore one mislaid tie to its owner, Tara Walsh, so impressed him that nothing would do him but to marry her. "Tara has to look after his own ties now though – I'm busy," she jokes, her hands full with six-month-old baby son, Ronan.

Joking aside, the ethos of doing more than is expected of you comes naturally to Caitriona and her colleagues at the Radisson SAS St Helen's Hotel in Stillorgan, south Dublin.

Caitriona is a rooms division manager – no small task in a five-star hotel with over 150 rooms – but she also makes time to look after the Corporate Social Responsibility programme and is programme co-ordinator for all the hotels in the Rezidor SAS chain in Ireland and the UK.

"Every hotel has got a charity dear to their heart and fundraises for that charity each year," she explains. "Each hotel also has an energy efficiency policy and an environmentally friendly policy. All these efforts combined make for a business that acts responsibly in society. In my role as co-ordinator, I keep an eye on how each hotel is living up to those responsibilities."

The chosen charity at St Helen's is Irish Guide Dogs for the Blind, a choice she thinks might have been inspired by her upbringing on a farm near Inver, Co Donegal, where she and her four brothers always counted dogs as part of the family.

Home also set an example for doing good. The McGroary children were brought up knowing the Little Way Association, the movement inspired by St Therese of Liseux's belief in doing ordinary things extraordinarily well.

"People at home were naturally charitable. My grandfather died of cancer at home in a livingroom converted to a bedroom and afterwards people fundraised to provide a coffee dock at the hospital so that family members wanting to stay with someone who was dying could get a cuppa and a bite to eat. I think it's an Irish thing – I don't think there is a person in Ireland who doesn't have a charity close to their heart."

At St Helen's, Caitriona and the staff have run quizzes and race nights to raise money and the hotel also hosts the launch of Shades Week, the annual national fundraising week of Irish Guide Dogs for the Blind.

"What we really love about Guide Dogs is that the people behind it are so sincere and inventive, and always looking to improve and develop. They make you want to be a better person. Our general manager was so impressed, he became a puppy walker, so it's rubbing off on all of us."

Caitriona and Ronan.

JOSEPHINE McKENNA
Donor

PERMANENT and pensionable were important words to a single woman in 1950s Ireland so Josephine McKenna quite enjoyed the minor scandal she caused when she left her sensible librarian's job for Canada.

It was only meant to be temporary, to help a sister over the death of her husband, but when she next packed her cases, seven years had passed and the destination was Zambia.

Zambia had just gained independence and a multinational effort was under way to build the new state. Josephine got a job as librarian at a fledgling law school and braced herself for a learning experience.

Her first lesson came quickly. She had arranged for her belongings to be shipped from Canada but a strike left her trunk stranded in port for six months so she arrived in Zambia with her wardrobe 7,000 miles away.

"I learned: always keep things simple. Luckily, it was the year of the shift dress. I bought slices of gorgeous cotton from the market, sewed up the two sides, left armholes and a gap for my head and voila – fashionable and cool!"

Josephine spent two happy years at the school before moving to the newly established parliament. She lived in a mud hut roofed with banana leaves, explored the vast Zambesi river and stunning Victoria Falls, and mixed with students, teachers, missionaries, diplomats, politicians and volunteers from all over the world.

Just as Zambia was finding its feet, so too were the people who came to help. "Everybody had to muck in and help each other. It was sharing in the truest sense. I learned that I don't care if some people have no shoes. I will kick off mine."

Josephine was sorry to leave and delayed her return home with a five-year stint at the European Commission in Brussels before coming back to the European Foundation in Dublin.

The teachings of Africa never left her, however, and in 2005, after two successful cataract operations, she made a decision she is certain had its roots in Zambia: she willed her investments and her home to Irish Guide Dogs for the Blind.

"I have often walked behind guide dogs on the street and it's magnificent to see the freedom that the person has. I see the dog with his tail upright and he is like a conductor with his baton, keeping perfect rhythm.

"In Africa we learned to make the best use of whatever we had. I want my investments and my house to work after I'm gone. I could leave everything to relatives but I thought: 'What will they do except maybe buy new cars?' Well, petrol is running out, but dogs aren't!

"My relatives are marvellous. Their attitude is that it's my life and my choice. Mother Africa taught me a lot – I just want the lesson to carry on."

PASCAL McNAMARA
Corporate social responsibility advocate

BUSINESS jargon was always a bit of a bore to Pascal McNamara. Say 'corporate social responsibility' to him and he struggled not to respond with a glance to heaven and a cavernous yawn.

That was until he met the Bogota-based chief executive of a multinational company who'd had both his thumbs hacked off by a Colombian kidnap gang.

"In Colombia, when companies talked about their annual report, they didn't mean their financial report. They meant their CSR report – corporate social responsibility," says Pascal, who was working for a Belgian business research firm at the time.

"Before they talked about profits, they had to show what they'd done for the community – how many hospitals or schools they provided. They did it out of fear because they were trying to avoid kidnapping."

Needless to say, when Pascal was back working in Ireland in the Merchants Group in Cork and a new company chairman started talking about CSR, he was intrigued to know if the staff were all in imminent danger of becoming ransom fodder.

"I kept asking him, why do you want to do something for the community? Why? Why? He eventually got quite annoyed and snapped: 'Because it's the right thing to do.' I couldn't argue with that."

Pascal was appointed CSR organiser and through a staff vote three charities were adopted, including Irish Guide Dogs for the Blind. Then they set about raising funds – and having fun.

"It was great. There were people you would see in the building but never spoke to who you were suddenly mixing with. You can be really surprised by who you have working for you.

"Every company has a Mary-the-tea-lady type figure. All you know is that Mary makes the tea because even though you've known her for years, you only ever say five sentences to her and they're invariably about the weather. Suddenly you're seeing the full Mary."

The staff started with simple but profitable projects like supermarket collections, flag days and jersey days. "It was a great shock to us to discover on jersey day that there were people in the company who were not from Cork. We'd been infiltrated by outsiders!"

Now working in recruitment, Pascal intends spreading the word about CSR. "Some companies do it because they figure it makes them look good. It still does some good but the motives are a bit questionable. But if you're doing it because it's the right thing to do, staff respond to that and it's a win-win situation. You won't find me arguing with that."

MICHAEL MEANY
Guide dog owner and former board member and chairman

MICHAEL Meany was afraid of dogs and couldn't quite believe it when he found himself at a training centre for blind people in England, face to face with a large, panting, sharp-toothed monster.

"He'll eat me," Michael yelled in panic as the beast probed him with an inquisitive nose and his hand fell on a 97lb German shepherd. "Not at all," came the reply from the amused trainer witnessing the scene. "We fed him this morning."

Still, Michael had to battle his nerves every day until the time he was sent to the kennels to fetch the monster himself. In their enthusiasm, six energetic guide dogs-in-training jumped up on him and knocked him flying.

When he emerged from under the melee of fur and fangs he found himself covered only in dog hairs and slobbery licks. So they really don't eat people, he reasoned. His liberation as a guide dog owner began. "From then on I was absolutely flying," he recalls.

Over a quarter of century later, Michael and Brady, the third successor to that first English companion, are inseparable and Michael likes nothing better than to calm nervous strangers by grinning mischievously and assuring them that his buddy isn't hungry.

Michael has lived in his native Limerick city for most of his life, apart from his time in special schools for the blind in Dublin where he was first sent at the tender age of five.

Separation from family was hard on one so young but he learned the skills of Braille, which allowed him to devour books and sparked a lifelong love of reading. He also learned touch typing which has allowed him to adapt with ease to the surge of new computer technology in recent years.

His only gripe about computers is that they make life too easy at times. He worked as a telephonist for the former Mid-Western Health Board for over 38 years, starting with three phone lines and 15 extensions and ending with 70 lines and 1,000 extensions, the majority of which Michael knew by heart.

"If I was there now, the computer would remember them for me and I wouldn't use my mind as much," he says. He even chides himself for using his electronic Braille diary which holds all his personal numbers. "I should really try to recall them myself."

Michael has no fear of his mind going into retirement mode, however, as he regularly plays chess, writes a web blog, sings and belts out countless accordion tunes.

It was at a wedding where the guests were dancing to Michael's accordion that he met his wife-to-be, Eileen. The couple celebrated their 40th wedding anniversary in 2006 along with their six children and 18 grandchildren.

With such a busy household, Michael never had time or the inclination to feel helpless or sorry for himself. "Eileen has always been brilliant but she had the children to look after and she works full time, so I just get on with it.

"I try to be a bit of help around the house but I'm like a lot of men – I'm not the best at housework. I get the bank statements and the bills in Braille so I can look after them and I know which ones to throw away!

"Some people treat you differently because you're blind but then some people can't handle disability. It's an ongoing education for the general public. I don't grumble about it."

Michael doesn't cycle now, though he previously pedalled along Australia's expansive east coast and from Hungary to Venice with the Blazing Saddles fundraising group, but he did learn to swim when he was in his forties and discovered a belated love of the water.

His piece de resistance, however, is learning to cook. Michael only recently returned to the Irish Guide Dogs for the Blind training centre to take a course in cookery with the independent living skills instructors.

"God bless them," Eileen declares. "It's great when I come home now and the dinner is cooked."

"I like to do it," Michael agrees. "But," he adds with a grin and a whisper as Eileen leaves to go to work, "it doesn't mean I've forgotten how to order a Chinese."

147

OLLIE MOONEY
Guide dog owner

THE last thing Ollie Mooney saw before his fading sight vanished was the televised funeral of US President John F Kennedy.

Glad to have witnessed a scene from history, his only regret is that the occasion was sad, for Ollie has always made a point of trying to see the funny side of life.

Ollie is in his 80th year and has been married to Rosaleen, who is also blind, since 1953. The pair first met when he was sent from his Co Offaly home, and she from her family in neighbouring Co Westmeath, to St Mary's School for blind children in Dublin.

"We met again years later at a National League of the Blind dance and I remembered her from school," Ollie says with a chuckle. Rosaleen smiles, knowing the punch-line that follows: "…only I didn't remember enough or I wouldn't have married her!"

Ollie retained some sight for a further 10 years and the couple busied themselves setting up home in Dublin where Ollie was employed as a mat maker and upholsterer and Rosaleen worked at knitting and bookbinding.

Their first home together was on Richmond Road, along the Tolka River, which burst its banks during the disastrous floods of 1954. "We lost everything we had," Rosaleen recalls. "All our wedding presents were floating up the street."

The corporation found them an upstairs flat in O'Devaney Gardens near the Phoenix Park where they lived until they retired and moved to their small bungalow a short distance away on the Navan Road where Ollie grows plants in pots in the tiny front garden and Rosaleen listens to the birds singing out the back.

"We always had good neighbours, here and in the flats," Rosaleen says. "They had the height of respect for us. Tiny little children would wave down the bus for us and the boys would always stop their football to let us pass. They were friends as well as neighbours."

A landmark part of their neighbourhood now is McKee Army Barracks and Ollie and his guide dog, Louis, have the honour of an anytime pass to the soldiers' mess. "It has the best value pint in Dublin," Ollie declares. "Maybe I shouldn't say that or they'll all want to come with me. I might find myself too popular!"

Rosaleen leaves himself and Louis to it. "He has enough girlfriends down there already," she teases.

While Ollie enjoys a pint and a chat, Louis gets a workout courtesy of the soldiers. "The lads bring him out for a run. They think the world of him. They even have a collection box they fill for Irish Guide Dogs for the Blind."

Louis is only Ollie's second guide dog. He had used a cane for so long that he didn't think he would adapt to a dog but he was thrilled with his new partner. "It used to be grand walking with the cane but there's too many poles and cars on the footpaths now. You wouldn't get 10 feet without walking into something if you didn't have the dog."

He and his first dog, Derry, almost wore a hollow in the path up and down to Hill Street to the National League of the Blind where Ollie worked for many years as long-serving president, advising members on employment opportunities and entitlements, and planning outings and events for the associated social club.

Rosaleen came late to mobility training, taking on the long cane. "We never heard of mobility training when we were young. You just had to get out and feel your way around. I often wonder how we survived at all."

Music is her great love and her big treat is a trip to the National Concert Hall or local musical society performances. "I always wanted to be a violinist," she says, "but I only got to play the knitting needles!"

The pair both love the radio and talking books. "I love romances," Ollie grins. "Don't mind him," says Rosaleen, "He's only teasing me. He likes the detective novels."
"She's right," Ollie chuckles. "I've too much romance in real life to bother with it in books."

BOB MURPHY
Guide dog owner and former board member

BOB Murphy thought his days of creating and constructing were over when his fading sight finally vanished in 1977.

For a long time the Co Wexford-born structural engineer had to put his ideas on the backburner while he adjusted to the changes blindness forced on him.

But now he is back in action, engineering a pioneering technology project for people with disabilities and building an ever-growing network of clients.

Bob works with the Health Service Executive in the north-west and from his base in Sligo he runs an Assistive Technology Unit catering for 250 people in counties Sligo, Donegal, Leitrim and parts of Cavan.

"We support people with disabilities using computer technology that's adapted to assist with the blind and visually impaired, hearing problems, people with speech difficulties, paralysis, dexterity problems – a whole range of different disabilities.

"The basic aim is to provide a means of communication but that can be communication for its own sake or for learning and work as well. We're also helping some children with learning disabilities and helping their schools too – the possibilities are endless."

Yet when Bob lost his sight, there didn't seem to be many possibilities – only improbabilities. Irish Guide Dogs for the Blind had not yet begun providing dogs and the only career path he could find was to train in telephony.

A vacancy for a telephonist brought him to the tax office in Sligo and, as soon as he could, Bob signed up for a guide dog which allowed him find his way both in his new surroundings and new life.

He still yearned to be exercising the skills he had honed in his sighted days, however, and, by his own admission, he pestered his employers to give him a computer even though he didn't need it for the job.

"I had to convince them but I find that if you're in any way reasonable with people, they will be reasonable with you. If you're a sullen, down-in-the-dumps sort of guy you can forget about it. They will give you back the same as you give them."

Bob got his computer and began experimenting with programmes and software until his proficiency got him noticed. The former North Western Health Board was beginning to fund assistive technology for clients in the region but could only provide the equipment, not the training, advice or back-up.

Before long, Bob had swapped wealth for health, leaving the tax office for the health board and getting to work building up the Assistive Technology Unit. He now has a staff of three technicians and a satellite unit in Letterkenny.

Bob has the technical expertise to assist clients but, crucially, he also has the insight into disability that allows him understand their needs, their ambitions and their frustrations.

"People get frustrated, not just with their disability but with the way they're treated because of their disability. For example, I don't like the term 'visually impaired'. At the end of the day I am blind. That's the fact of the matter and to hell with it. The flowery words don't take away from the fact that I am blind. People don't want you to skirt around their disability. They want you to deal with it."

Bob spent 12 years as a board member of Irish Guide Dogs for the Blind and he remains an active branch member. When he has free time, he tinkers about with DIY, roars from the sideline at GAA matches, roars at the television during Liverpool games or simply enjoys the company of his wife Helen, children Ruaidhri and Aisling, and Anna, his third guide dog.

"There isn't a lot of free time because my hope now is to expand units right throughout the west into Galway, Mayo and Clare. There is a hell of a lot of work to do. I have plenty of dreams."

Bob with Guide Dog Anna.

151

MAY MURPHY
Guide dog owner and former board member

LONG commutes are not just a modern phenomenon: when May Murphy was at work, just getting to and from the office was a job in itself.

She began with a walk, then a bus, another walk, a second bus and then completed the final stretch on foot, before facing into the same trek on the way home. What's more, she did it all under the curious eyes of the public, as May was the first female guide dog owner in Ireland.

It's a little piece of history that she is proud to have created, not least because her first dog marked the start of 40 years of successful partnerships with guide dogs that only ended in 2000.

"I was 74 and I wasn't fit enough any more, so I hung up my boots. A dog needs someone to give them a good run and I was a bit beyond running. It was lonely at first but I had built up hobbies when I had dogs and I kept them up, so I'm still getting the benefit out of them."

May was born in Dundalk, Co Louth, and attended St Mary's School for blind girls in Dublin before training in England as a telephonist. On her return home, she worked in an employment exchange and the old St Kevin's Hospital in Dublin before a position cropped up with Irish Shell at the docks.

"I felt protected in the hospital setting and now I was going to a commercial firm and I was terrified," she recalls. "I thought they would be hard on me. But one of the first things the management did was encourage me to get a guide dog."

The company gave May time off in 1960 to go to England to train with a dog and she returned with Trudy. At the time she lived in digs in Rathmines on the southside and it was difficult undertaking the epic journey to work each day with her new companion.

"In the beginning I was terrified. My sister used to say I was like a mother with a first child – I was afraid the dog would break! But after about six months I was walking faster and soon we were flying along.

"I had wonderful walks with Trudy. That's the joy of a dog. I remember the first St Patrick's weekend with her, I just remember the feeling of, 'This is really good, I am really delighted with this'."

Dusty followed Trudy, and May continued her trek across the city each day until her brother urged her to visit him in the United States. "I had bad habits," she laughs. "I smoked and I never saved. But I gave up smoking to pay for the trip and I was surprised at how much money I saved so I thought maybe I could save to buy a house."

In 1976, May and Dusty moved to Clontarf, much closer to the docks, and May has called it home ever since. "It's more like a village than part of the city. People know each other. They leave me across the road and then people in the shop leave me back. A neighbour gives me a lift to Mass every morning. I'm very happy here."

Three more guide dogs, Cherry, Janette and Lass, shared May's home and she has fond memories of each one.

"Each dog coincided with a new phase in my life. I learnt it all with Trudy and I got even more independent with Dusty when I got my own home. Then Cherry brought me into my new life, my retirement.

"I use the long cane now but I miss what a dog can do for me. You can speed along and the dog will bring you around the obstacles. With the stick, you have to find the obstacles and get around them and my goodness, the paths have a lot of obstacles now with poles and electricity boxes and parked cars.

"But even now I often think of lovely sunny mornings walking down East Wall Road. I always thought it was a wonderful sense of freedom. I still have that feeling in my mind."

May Murphy receiving a bouquet from Emily Daly, Cobh, on the occasion of the opening by May of the "Tribute Garden" at the National Headquarters & Training Centre, Cork (September 2nd, 2006).

OLIVIA MUSGRAVE
Sculptor

SCULPTOR Olivia Musgrave draws inspiration from the characters and creatures of Greek mythology – tales that have survived through millennia.

When she took on the task of sculpting for the memorial garden at the headquarters of the Irish Guide Dogs for the Blind, she was determined this piece too would tell a story that would stand the test of time.

The obvious choice for the commission was a guide dog owner and dog but Olivia decided straight away that the human figure should not be obviously blind and the dog should have no harness.

"I wanted to do something that represented the relationship between man and dog. Blindness wasn't the key issue: the relationship was. The relationship is about so much more than blindness – it's about trust and understanding and interdependence."

The resulting life-size bronze sculpture of man and dog walking side by side was appropriately named 'As One' and stands as a focal point of the garden where trainees, staff and volunteers alike can take time out from their tasks and sit and reflect on what their efforts are all about.

Having chosen her subject, Olivia had another decision to make. For her, the relationship between humans and animals is a story that predates known history and will endure until the end of time; if 'As One' was to convey that theme convincingly, it had to be a timeless piece. Put in a non-artistic way, the male figure had to be nude.

"I was worried at the unveiling about the fact that he didn't have any clothes on. The thing is, as soon as you put clothes on a figure, it really dates it, and this piece wasn't about a single event or a moment in time, it was about an eternal theme. I think there were some nuns at the unveiling and there might have been a few gasps when the cloth was pulled away! But generally the reaction has been really good."

Olivia, who was born in Dublin to an Irish father and Greek mother, spent several years travelling before settling in London where she enrolled in art college. Her story since has been one of steadily growing success. Still based in London, she works with the John Martin Gallery in Mayfair but she also exhibits in Dublin at the Royal Hibernian Academy and Jorgensen Fine Art.

Her biggest coup to date – both in terms of size and public profile – was a commission from the city of Oxford to create a full-size ox to stand outside Oxford Railway Station, but 'As One' holds a special place in her portfolio.

"I was particularly pleased that the money for it was raised separately. I really didn't want it to come from Guide Dogs' regular funds but it actually attracted more donations that it needed, so it has created its own momentum. That makes it quite special."

GER O'BYRNE
Supporter

SOME people like working with machines because they don't answer back. Others hate them for the same reason.

Ger O'Byrne was an electronic engineer who got far more enjoyment talking to the people whose appliances he fixed than he did from fixing the appliances, so he went back to college at night and emerged six years later with a masters degree in marketing.

It took him to a job where he has the potential to communicate with every single person in the country because Ger works with An Post as product manager in charge of direct mail for all of Ireland.

The job got him meeting new faces in another unexpected way. Retired colleague, Ben Kenny, is a board member of Irish Guide Dogs for the Blind and, while chatting one day, told Ger of his work with the organisation.

Ger was fascinated and vowed to get involved but his chance came in an unlikely way after a hip replacement operation in 2005. His favourite hobby was scuba diving and he loved the waters off Fanore in the Burren. The surgery ruled out diving for the year but when he saw that Irish Guide Dogs for the Blind had a 100-kilometre fundraising trek through the Burren, he immediately signed up.

"I met amazing people from all walks of life. You're talking as you're walking every day and in the evenings you sit down and talk some more. Most of these people were involved in Guide Dogs far longer than me, in all sorts of ways, and they're very driven. I wondered why people do this. What drives them? But they don't think it's a big deal at all. They just say, sure what else would I be doing? Watching the telly or down the pub."

Ger could just as easily be asked what drives him. As well as Irish Guide Dogs for the Blind, the native Dubliner has fundraised for the hospice service in his adopted Co Meath and he is PRO, website director and database manager for Ratoath GAA Club.

"We have 55 teams, 2000 members and a mortgage of €2m because we just opened a new clubhouse. It keeps us on our toes," he says with understatement.

The O'Byrne household is also busy. Mum, Brid, is a theatre nurse, and children, 15-year-old Ronan and 12-year-old Ciara, have packed schedules which include play time for Rusty, the family's beloved collie who was rescued from an abusive home.

"We're the typical modern family – both parents working, commuting – all of that, and it is a lifestyle that makes it hard to find time for voluntary work. But you can fit a bit in and you get great satisfaction out of it. If 20 people all do a little bit, that's a lot of work altogether. It's also very sociable and I really like that part."

Ger, Ronan, Brid and Ciara.

156

JULIE O'CARROLL
Guide dog owner

JULIE O'Carroll can only smile to herself when she hears parents complaining that they need eyes in the back of their head.

Julie is a single parent of five and she just happens to be blind.

"I thought I'd have an operation and I'd be grand," she says of the sight problems that left her prone to tripping over stray Hoovers and other unexpected obstacles left sitting out around the hotel where she worked.

When the doctor diagnosed her with retinitis pigmentosa and told her she would lose her sight, she was devastated. "I bawled my eyes out and the young nurse who was there started crying too. It was awful."

She wasn't crying just for herself, but also for her children, Richard, Stephen, Amanda and Jacqueline, as she couldn't imagine how she would look after them. The baby of the family, Eric, wasn't even born at the time.

Julie trained to use a long cane first but hesitated about actually using it. "I remember my trainer saying that he didn't want to call around to the house and find the cane hanging up behind the door with a 'Break in case of emergency' sign on it. Of course, I did leave it hanging on the door - until I got fed up getting bumps and bruises."

She felt her older children would be embarrassed that their mother was a cane user but she reasoned that being embarrassed by one's parents was a normal feature of teenage life and decided to get on with it.

"Eric grew up not knowing any different so he was fine. When he was a toddler he would hear me coming and shout: 'Mam, I'm on the floor!'. I stood on his poor fingers so many times he knew he either had to warn me where he was or get out of the way fast!"

Eric provided the impetus for Julie to get a guide dog. "I wanted to be able to walk him to school when he started. That was one of the first things I wanted to do when I trained with Nessa."

Nessa was Julie's first guide dog and together they did practice runs up and down to school during the summer to make sure they were ready for Eric's big day but it was still daunting when the time arrived.

"Eric was only starting school and he had other children asking him what was wrong with his mother. But it would have been worse if I hadn't had the independence to take my own son to school. We said it'll work itself out and it did. The other kids don't take any notice now."

Nessa is retired now but still lives in the family's Cork city home and is happy to let her successor, Quincy, take over the reins. The other family pet is mongrel Zoe who has learnt some guide dog traits just by watching, but apart from having exceptional dogs, the family is like any other.

"The children don't get any extra chores to do because of me, except for the shopping. The dog is marvellous but not quite good enough to do the shopping. But I do the rest. It's no different from any other household with children - none of them knows how to work the washing machine!"

There are times, however, when even Julie's best efforts can have hit-and-miss results.
"We went out to watch my brother play darts one day and we had our dinner out and he got sausage and chips. Amanda shouted, oh mam, he's eating raw sausage. My brother said: 'That's how sausages are supposed to look - your mam burns them!'"

"When Eric was very small we had a smoke alarm that was quite sensitive and when it would go off he'd say: 'Mam, the dinner's ready'."

Julie reckons it was their unique dining experiences that prompted both her older sons to train as chefs.

"They were so fed up of eating burnt food that they said they better learn to cook themselves! It's no harm – it'll make them more independent than a lot of young fellas their age."

Julie, daughter Jacqueline and Guide Dog Quincey.

TIM O'CONNELL
Visiting teacher

TIM O'Connell's ambition was always to work himself out of a job.

He was one of the country's first batch of 'visiting teachers', responsible for supporting blind and visually impaired children in mainstream schools.

It was 1979 when he started and almost all blind children were being sent as boarders to two schools in Dublin: St Mary's for the girls and St Joseph's for the boys. Tim's job was to help keep children living at home and attending their local schools.

Change didn't happen overnight but now practically all children are in mainstream education and can avail of many supports.

"I'd meet the child and talk to the school and ask what they need. Then I'd organise computers, laptops, speech software, typing tuition, resource teaching hours, classroom assistants – whatever was needed," he explains.

No computer will listen like a human can, however, so spending time with parents and children is still a hugely important part of the visiting teacher's work.

"I have eaten a world of apple tarts in family kitchens down over the years and between the chats about the weather and the farm and whatever else, I've got to hear about parents' fears and their concerns.

"There is a cycle you can almost predict when parents find out their child won't see. It takes three to four years to come to terms with it. There's denial, the search for a cure, and then acceptance of reality.

"To get through to parents is essential. There's a world of difference now in terms of the impact of blindness. I often quote David Blunkett. He said: "I don't regard it as a handicap at all or a disability but an occasional inconvenience.

"I've had kids who are absolutely brilliant and living hugely successful lives. Blind people now are lawyers, interpreters, IT specialists. Parents ask what will their child be able to do. I tell them anything really."

Tim, who lives in Dripsey, Co Cork, was very involved in getting Department of Education recognition and funding for the independent living skills courses now taught by Irish Guide Dogs for the Blind.

"We argued there was no point in the department giving blind students the means academically to get into college if they couldn't physically look after themselves when they got there!"

He didn't quite work himself out of a job as retirement got in the way, but he's now working part-time teaching young teachers at University College Cork.

"It will happen that schools don't need outside help in catering for a child with a disability because teachers will automatically be trained and equipped to do it," he says confidently. "That's when my job will finally be done."

Eileen and Tim O Connell.

ANNE O'FARRELLL & ANNETTE HARTE
Fundraisers

LAUGHTER may be the best medicine but for Anne O'Farrell and Annette Harte, generosity makes an excellent tonic too.

The fundraising friends from Bishopstown, Cork, have found a niche for themselves setting up stalls for Irish Guide Dogs for the Blind in the city's main hospitals and the warmth of the reception they get never ceases to amaze them.

"People in hospitals have other things on their mind. They might be worried about themselves or someone they're visiting. But they're unbelievably generous. They love to see the Guide Dogs stall," says Anne.

"The patients come down to see us. It's a good excuse for them to get a wander away from the ward," says Annette. "The staff are brilliant too and people visiting always come over for a look. We never have to go after them."

The stall sells whatever is the latest gift or practical item from an expanding range of goodies. Umbrellas are popular given the Irish weather and cards, calendars and stationery always go well but the undisputed top seller is the cute and cuddly soft toy labrador.

"We can't get enough of those dogs," Annette laughs. "I think a lot of them end up on the wards keeping the patients company and not just on the children's wards either."

Anne, a Cork native, and Annette, who is originally from Derry but has honorary Corkwoman status after 40 years in the city and marriage to a Corkman, together make up one-third of the Bishopstown branch and have about 50 years' involvement between them.

"We're small but we're strong," says Anne. "We don't do much but what we do, we put our hearts and souls into."

"We are very, very lucky with all the people involved. All the members are marvellous and we have friends and family we can call on when we have a flag day or church gate collection."

In return for their efforts, they find Irish Guide Dogs for the Blind fosters friendships and teamwork.

"We found we worked very well together. We have the same way of thinking – that people will support your cause if you are pleasant and friendly to them," says Annette. "And not too pushy," Ann agrees.

But the real reward, they say, is seeing the organisation grow and strengthen over the years.

"I remember when we came out here first," Annette says of the National Headquarters and Training Centre. "There was a leak in the roof and staff sitting inside in their anoraks. It's amazing what they have done and it's a credit to the generosity of ordinary people. It does you good to see it."

Betty Flanagan,
Annette Harte,
Denis Collins,
Anne O'Farrell,
Peggy O'Leary
and Eileen Harris

BETTY O'LEARY
Fundraiser

AT first glance, Betty O'Leary's diary made her appear an insatiable socialite. The Listowel Races, Rose of Tralee, Munster Final – wherever a crowd gathered, Betty was in its midst.

Other venues suggested a different explanation. After all, cattle marts and the pavement outside Dunnes Stores were hardly the most glamorous of places.

Betty mixed with race-goers, revellers, housewives, horse owners, farmers and football fans with equal enthusiasm and with one goal – to introduce them to her collection bucket for Irish Guide Dogs for the Blind.

The organisation has been hugely important in the O'Leary household in Killarney since one of the 10 O'Leary children, also called Betty and now a barrister based in Dublin, got her first dog in 1992.

Betty senior raised funds while her late husband, Sean, raised pups. But during a big match they worked together, Sean manning a designated safe house where the buckets could be emptied and the money stored until the game was over.

"Sean would always offer to mind the money," says Betty senior. "The only way he would get to see the whole match was to be inside with the television!"

Sean took the breeding duties very seriously and would set up a video camera linked to a television in the bedroom so he wouldn't miss a new arrival if an expectant mum gave birth at night. He was equally devoted to puppy-walking and cared for nine young prospective guide dogs until it was time for them to leave for training.

"Dad loved them. You got a little ball of fluff, barely weaned, completely clumsy and sticking its paws in its food bowl; and eight months later you gave back a dog ready to be trained as a guide dog," Betty junior says.

He would always claim to be happy to see them go but his affection for them, and all animals, was obvious. During Christmas 2005, weeks before his death, a small grey cat appeared in the yard and he anguished over leaving it outside in the cold in the hope that it would return to a probably fretting owner.

After a few days he found the creature sleeping under the car engine and decided it was better that an owner fret than a cat freeze. Smokey, as he called the little bundle, keeps his rocking chair warm since he died.

Family and friends struggled to find words warm enough to honour Sean when he passed away but they were saved by Betty's guide dog, Benny.

"He stayed by Dad's coffin for two days and then when it came time to close it and we all stood around not knowing who should say goodbye first, Benny stood up and leaned over the coffin and laid his head against Dad. It was a lovely tribute, as fitting as anything we could do."

AEDAN O'MEARA
Long cane user

WHEN Aedan O'Meara announced plans to buy and restore a ruined old farmhouse, polite coughs covered up for listeners' disbelief.

Aedan understands the scepticism. As he admits of his rural West Cork retreat: "There was a foot of earth in the kitchen you could grow spuds in. There was a tree growing in through the hall door and six inches of cow dung on the sitting room floor. The floorboards were mushy and the ceiling timbers were crumbling. It wasn't in great shape."

That was 1989, and he has spent most of his spare time since then performing minor miracles on the apparently hopeless house. Now it's his own little piece of heaven.

"I love the isolation. I love the birds, the bees, the dogs barking in the distance; the smell of the sea and Galley Head lighthouse lighting up our bedroom window at night; the wind in the trees and the wash of the water over the pebbles and the crash of waves in rough weather; the cock pheasant in the field beside us, the swallows in the eves … it's magic."

What makes it all the more magical for Aedan is that he did practically all the work himself. "The family got hammers and beat all the mortar off the walls back to bare stone but I cut every bit of timber myself.

"I did all the plumbing and electrical work as well. My wife, Barbara, told me the colour of the wires but I did all the rest myself and got my RECI (Register of Electrical Contractors of Ireland) cert for the work without any problem. I also poured cement by hand from a bucket with rubber gloves.

"I still don't know how I drive a nail in without hitting my thumb but they tell me there is a memory muscle so your hand repeats an action correctly – once you concentrate enough to do it correctly to start with!

"I get migraines from concentrating and visualising all the time. That house is built on ferocious concentration and migraines."

Aedan, a Dubliner by birth and a vet by training, moved to Cork in 1973 to take up an office post with the Department of Agriculture, where he still works.

He lost his sight gradually to retinitis pigmentosa but retains strong visual memories that keep him tinkering about with DIY, science projects and even car maintenance.

He marvels at the trust Barbara and their son and four daughters place in him: "Barbara's even lets me do the brakes on the car. I mean - I wouldn't let a blind man do the brakes on my car!"

Others aren't always so relaxed and he recalls a neighbour complaining that she couldn't sunbathe in peace because Aedan was on the roof fixing something and her heart was missing beats for fear he would fall.

The roof is a favourite place for Aedan, who is also ham radio fanatic. He speaks of magnetic loop aerials, microwaves and satellite receivers like he's scripting a science fiction movie and he once, during a casual twiddle of his dials, made contact with the Mir space station.

His licensed call-sign is EI3EG and he could barely believe it one Sunday morning when he found Mir acknowledging his message. "If I'd registered for my call-sign earlier I'd have got EI2EG which could have stood for Ireland – Two Eyes Gone," he jokes. "I'm sorry I missed that."

Aedan says he looks at blindness as a challenge and the explorer in him probes his surroundings, terrestrial and celestial, with equal zeal.

"I've had four guide dogs and I might go back to a dog some day but for the moment I'm using the cane. The cane is slower but I like the contact it gives me with my environment. It's me finding my own way.

"I'm a bit of a philosopher. I think of the first men in space as the equivalent of fish in a fish tank, who have jumped out of the tank and are looking back at it from a distance and seeing it clear and complete for the first time.

"I'm looking back at my sighted days from a distance but I can still see clearly in that sense. You don't come to that way of thinking easily. There are all these layers of admission and acceptance to go through. People come to it in their own time. You can't force it."

Barbara and Aedan.

TOM & BREEGE O'NEILL
Former board member and guide dog owners

TOM O'Neill acquired many skills in his life but the one he mastered best was denial.

Although born with progressively fading eyesight, he didn't think twice about signing up for driving lessons in the belief that he could motor around the children in the residential care centre in Galway where he worked.

He even went for a job with a textile firm which he was assured was his so long as he wasn't colourblind. Colourblindness was the least of his worries, for Tom could barely see at all.

For years he never even told his family in neighbouring Co Mayo about his predicament and says without bitterness that his expertise in denial was an inherited trait.

"Our granny sat by the fire all the time and we thought that's what grannies did. Nobody said she's there because she's blind. My granny was blind, my mother was blind, as well as one uncle and his sister; but to this day this generation are uncomfortable talking about it. I planned to carry on that tradition."

But Tom's plans came unravelled when he met Tom Langan, a guide dog owner who worked as a telephonist with the health board in Galway. Tom persuaded his namesake to face up to his situation and the master of denial moved to Sligo to train in Braille and telephony.

Once he got there, there was no turning back because that's where Tom met Breege. After some long distance romancing, the couple married in 1980 and both secured jobs with the Revenue Commissioners in Dublin.

Breege still had some vision at the time and with long canes they commuted from their home in Balbriggan, north Co Dublin, to the city centre each day. But baby Laura was born in 1982 and Eoin followed in 1983 and suddenly Tom was without Breege's help to get around.

"I still didn't want a guide dog. I used to get on the train each morning, fold up the cane, put it in my pocket and pretend I was like anybody else.

The drawback of a guide dog was that I couldn't hide it in my pocket but eventually I was convinced to apply."

Even then, he found the process tough. Tom was called to train with his dog while Breege was undergoing surgery in England and it all became too much.

"I was down in Cork trying to run a home from a coin box and I felt I'd had enough. I started to pack my bag to leave but I stopped and said to myself: 'You are in denial, you have always been in denial. You have to pull yourself together, think of the children, think of Breege. Your mobility is a means to an end. It's a means to your mortgage. It's a roof over your family's head. You have to get on with it'."

Tom unpacked and didn't leave again until Frank, his first dog, was by his side. Tom realised he'd finally left behind the 'denial years', as he calls them, one morning when he called Frank in from the garden and he didn't appear.

Tom rang neighbours, friends and the local schools, hoping that one of the teachers, children or bus drivers might have spotted him. Soon most of Balbriggan was on the lookout.

Poor Frank, meanwhile, had only wandered yards away but managed to get himself locked in the back garden of a neighbour who had gone to work. When the emergency was over, Tom could only laugh: there were no more secrets – everyone knew he was blind. The next time such a crowd came out for Frank was when he retired and a huge ceremony was held to bestow on him the honour of 'Freedom of the lamp-posts of Balbriggan'.

Since then, Tom has had Bruce and Kola to guide him while Breege also applied and has had Gypsie, Abbie and Unice.

"A lot of people have come around us in the community," says Breege. "We were always this novelty blind couple and maybe people felt a bit awkward towards us, but now we're a couple with a pair of dogs and that's a great ice-breaker. We're still a bit of a novelty but at least neither of us is trying to hide who we are."

Tom and Guide Dog Kola, Breege and Guide Dog Unice.

DR ARTHUR O'REILLY
Board member

THE United Nations conjures up images of powerful countries, influential heads of state, and issues of such gravitas and complexity that the input of the ordinary citizen is irrelevant.

But on its agenda is a proposal that proves people power can still make waves.

That proposal has become the Convention on the Rights of People with Disabilities which, when adopted, will bind signatory countries to protect and assert the rights of all individuals with a disability that threatens to exclude them from participating fully in life.

The record books will show that this historic piece of international legislation got on to the UN's crammed agenda through the efforts of Dr Arthur O'Reilly.

In 1999, as director of the National Disability Authority and president of disability rights group Rehabilitation International, Arthur brought the idea to the UN's attention. Progress has been slow but, Arthur says, well worth the wait.

Career paths can follow straight lines or zig-zag from one direction to another. Arthur chose the latter and has enjoyed an ever-changing scenery.

Psychology was his first love and his studies earned him a doctorate but the academic life was not for him and he took a job with An Foras Taluntais, the forerunner of Teagasc, the agricultural research authority. From there he moved to Anco, which became Fas, the national training and employment body, and later he switched to the National Rehabilitation Board, which evolved into the National Disability Authority.

Some would find the constant change unsettling but to Arthur it was stimulating and it was one of the reasons that, when he retired in 2001, he accepted an invitation to join the board of Irish Guide Dogs for the Blind.

"I wouldn't have been interested in getting involved in an organisation if it wasn't interested in moving forward," he explains. "I have no great interest in maintaining things. I am better at getting things started and moving them forward."

He felt Irish Guide Dogs for the Blind was of a similar mindset and believes the expansion in the scope and scale of the organisation's operations in recent years proved his instinct correct.

But, he says, there is more change required and more new routes to explore. He would like to see Irish Guide Dogs for the Blind take a leading role in promoting eye health – an area of healthcare he believes is badly neglected. He also believes the organisation can be a more vocal lobby on disability issues in general and that, with the right pitch, Government would be forced to take notice.

"It's hard work for an organisation that's already busy fulfilling its primary functions but if we can get the UN to take heed, surely we can be heard in Leinster House too."

MAY OSBURNE
Puppy walker, brood bitch holder and fundraiser

TIPTOE, scamper, run – these are the three stages familiar to every breeder of puppies and they apply to their human minders as much as the dogs.

The first stage, May Osburne explains, involves delicately stepping around the whelping box, the professional term for a birthing bed.

"The waiting is very stressful. You have the due arrival dates but you can't be exactly sure when the mother will deliver. You're always watching to see if anything is stirring. Of course, the very time you turn your back is when it's likely to start – then or in the early hours of the morning!"

Stage two is when the puppies arrive and duty calls for continuous scurrying back and forth to check the tiny bundles are feeding, growing and gaining strength. Stage three is when it's time to let them explore their new world – and when a puppy breeder needs their running shoes.

"The first few weeks, they are so quiet and then you take them out in the garden and suddenly you have puppies going off in all directions," says May, who has found herself chasing in 10 directions at once. "You always hope for a big litter but 10 is rather a lot!"

At six weeks the puppies leave to live with puppy walkers, another role well known to May. "They're pulling on the lead and dancing around your feet to start with, but hopefully after 10 months you have a lovely, obedient, sociable puppy."

By this stage, you also have a doting puppy walker and May admits it can be hard to say goodbye. "You've got them to the point where they're ready to train as a guide dog and you have to let them go. That's what you've both been preparing for."

Even when she hasn't a litter or a puppy to walk, May's home is not without the sound of padding paws because her constant companion is labrador Hester, her fundraising partner.

Together they run moneyspinners for Irish Guide Dogs for the Blind, including race nights, pitch and putt competitions and an annual sponsored dog walk in lovely Farran Wood near their home at Coachford, Co Cork.

May is also a regular on the "late running" roster where volunteers come to the kennels at the National Headquarters and Training Centre in the evening to give the dogs in training a pre-bedtime runaround and cuddle.

"It is a lot of work, I suppose, but it's wonderful for me, being on my own, because I never really am on my own. This really is my second family and when you see your dog working and their new owner smiling, that's all the thanks I want."

May with Hester.

THE O'SHEA FAMILY
Assistance dog programme participants

FIVE-year-old Sarah sits with her family, working her way through a packet of chocolate buttons and fingering the keys on her Bob the Builder telephone while cups of coffee and sandwiches are passed around the table.

All around her there are crowds and noise but Sarah is not bothered by the bustle. It is the most ordinary of scenes from a family day out but for the O'Sheas, moments like this were unimaginable a year and a half earlier.

"She would be taking this place apart by now," says dad, Brian, watching his little daughter looking around her contentedly. "We just couldn't be here."

The O'Sheas, from Midleton, Co Cork, were among the first three families in Ireland to take part in the assistance dog programme developed here by Irish Guide Dogs for the Blind from a model pioneered in Canada. The programme trains dogs to be guardians to autistic children and the results have been remarkable.

Sarah was just three at the time, making her the youngest child in the world to be approved for the programme, but already Brian and her mum, Noelle, were at their wit's end trying to care for her.

"Life was very stressful," Brian says. "Bringing Sarah out in public was extremely traumatic for her and equally so for us. We couldn't function properly as a family. One of us always had to stay at home. If we went to a family party or gathering, it was on the basis that, five minutes after we arrived, one of us would bring Sarah home."

Sarah's reaction when Eve arrived was instantly different to her usual response to a new arrival. "I would describe it as curiosity at a distance," says Brian of the first meeting between child and dog. "Normally, when someone new came into the house there'd be a tantrum, but Eve wasn't a person and Sarah wasn't troubled by her.

"Within a week there was a difference in her behaviour. The first time we took Sarah out with Eve we went to the shopping centre, which would normally have been a complete sensory overload for Sarah. We had the trainers with us on the day and they said they wanted us to stop for a cup of coffee. We said, lads, you're nuts! But we tried it and Sarah sat there quite happy. After that any time we passed a coffee shop, she wanted to go in."

Brian believes the sense of security Eve provides is pivotal to Sarah's progress. "I would describe Eve as Sarah's bodyguard. She is never more than four feet away from Sarah when they're out and that gives Sarah confidence so she doesn't get so stressed."

For the first year, Eve had more interest in Sarah than Sarah could reciprocate but slowly that changed. "Sarah's relationship with Eve at home was unusual. Eve served a purpose – she let Sarah walk in public – and the rest of the time Sarah ignored her. But slowly a bond developed. Now Sarah is hugging Eve, petting her, climbing on top of her. She has very limited vocabulary but she knows how to say, "I want Eve". She is a lot calmer, a lot more settled and happy."

Noelle echoes that view and is delighted that Sarah's six-year-old brother, Adam, can at last leave the house with both his parents. "We can do much more as a family. We can go away for a weekend, which we couldn't think about before. We're also able to expose Sarah to so much more of life, which is important because children with autism can get very set in their ways."

Eve has an expected working life of around seven years, so there is uncharted territory ahead when she retires, but the O'Sheas are happy to take one step at a time.

"We'll get a replacement if we need to but maybe, hopefully, Sarah won't need an assistance dog then and Eve could become her companion. These are things we're going to have to find out. All we know is that, before, we had no options; now, we can look ahead knowing the progress that Sarah has made and believing there's no reason it won't continue."

Noelle and John O Shea with daughter Sarah, son Adam and Assistance Dog Eve

JOHN O'SHEA
Fundraiser

JOHN O'Shea is proud of the medals that hang on his wall tracing his 21 years of service with the Irish Defence Forces.

Most treasured are the ones that mark his tour of duty with the United Nations peace-keepers in the Congo during turbulent times in the 1960s. He keeps them neatly framed and dusted and casts an eye over them every day. But these days invisible accolades mean just as much.

In fundraising for Irish Guide Dogs for the Blind, John has manned stalls outside supermarkets, shaken buckets, organised collection boxes, run raffles, and decorated countless sitting rooms at Christmas thanks to the berry-laden holly boughs he supplied in return for donations.

"Such a simple thing, yet people went mad for it. They couldn't get enough of it. I had to stop in the end because I was afraid of starving the birds of their winter feed," he laughs.

His association with Irish Guide Dogs for the Blind began simply too. He spotted one of the labrador-shaped collection boxes in a skip at a dump one day and brought it to work where it quickly filled up.

John contacted staff at the organisation, who were glad to relieve him of the box and he thought that was that. But they promptly sent him another one. And another. "It went from there. Before you know it, you have 40 boxes on the go."

John loves to be active, so it came as a fright when he suddenly found himself at a standstill after becoming seriously ill. But the ordeal made him more determined to squeeze all he could out of life.

"When I came out of hospital I couldn't walk. Then I walked on two sticks, then one, and eventually I got going on my own. That's when I got Ben."

Ben is the family pet and not surprisingly is a labrador although his immense size suggests he is at least half polar bear. "I often think he would be great to pull a sleigh," John jokes, thinking of the crucifying climbs up the steeply sloping streets of his hometown, Cobh.

As it is, John provides the chauffeur service and it is Ben who sits back in the family car, taking in the views and enjoying the ride. "We go all over the countryside together. He's great company. I think dogs surpass humans at times, they are so intelligent.

"Since my illness, I've been thinking every day how lucky I am. It's great to be alive. It's little enough to ask that I lend a hand to help someone else who might be having a tougher time.

"There are no medals for it at the end of the day, but I know it's important and it's appreciated. That's all that matters."

CHRISTINE O'SULLIVAN
Puppy walker and fundraiser

CHRISTINE O'Sullivan's husband gets nervous any time she mentions hairdressers.

If she ever runs out of ideas for fundraising, she intends organising a sponsored head shave, with her own long locks the first for the scissors.

It all started when Christine was puppy walking her second pup for Irish Guide Dogs for the Blind. Harmony, a lively black labrador, bolted out on to the normally quiet road beyond the front garden one day. The motorist who hit her didn't have a chance to stop.

When Christine rang headquarters to tell them of Harmony's death, she couldn't speak through her tears and husband, Paddy, had to take over.

When she eventually found her voice, she insisted they take money for the dog. They insisted they wouldn't. She insisted she had to do something to make it up to them. They sent her a bouquet of flowers.

It made matters worse, in the nicest possible way. "This huge bunch of flowers arrived and I started bawling again. It only made me more determined to try and pay them back.

"I was racking my brain trying to think of something to do to raise money and I said 'I'll do a head shave', but my husband put his foot down and said he'd be filing for divorce. I didn't want to lose a husband as well as the dog."

She organised a bed push instead, managing to coax local politicians on to the pillows for the trip from Kilgarvan to her home in Kenmare at the start of the Ring of Kerry. It was a great success and started the ball rolling on her fundraising endeavours.

As a child growing up in Tralee, Christine was fascinated by a local woman and her guide dog. Years later, a newspaper advertisement seeking people to puppy walk brought back those memories.

She signed up, much to the delight of her four children. "They're mad about the puppies. We try to bring them up not to be jealous children and the puppies remind them what's important.

"Your kids aren't really yours, they're only on loan while you're preparing them for a grown-up life and you have to enjoy them while you have them. It's the same with the dogs. The only difference is, even when the kids have left home, I hope I'll still be pottering around the road with dogs."

Christine's most ambitious 'potter' to date was her 26-mile walk of the New York City Marathon in aid of research into motor neuron disease. She hopes to do it again in 2007 for Irish Guide Dogs for the Blind – but she still insists she's keeping the head shave in reserve.

Back Row: Sons Padraig and Flor with Paddy. Front Row: Daughters Eilish and Orla with Christine and Guide Dog Puppy Orchid.

MARK O'SULLIVAN
Board member, financial advisor

IT'S a cliché that businessmen do their best work on the golf course, but on the first Friday of each September Mark O'Sullivan is happy to be stereotyped.

His annual fundraising golf competition for Irish Guide Dogs for the Blind has been running for 26 years without fail and each one rates on his score card as a good day's work.

Most of the contestants are returnees who come to the Monkstown Golf Club venue in Cork each year to resume old rivalries and chase the customary first prize of a case of wine as eagerly as if it were gold bullion.

"It has prestige value now. We've had a teetotaller win it recently and even he was delighted," says Mark.

There are 'ghost players' on the greens too – people who pay the entry fee but take no tee time in return. The most spectre-like of all is the main sponsor of the past three years who insists on anonymity.

"It's someone who nice and quietly wants to help. They're not into it to get their mugshot in the paper."

Mark was roped into organising the first competition by a friend of his father but over the years he became increasingly involved with Irish Guide Dogs for the Blind and in 2001 he joined the board.

As company secretary with an investments advisory firm, his expertise in money matters is invaluable and he sits on the finance subcommittee that aims to make the best out of every euro and cent that rolls in.

"We do an Eddie Hobbs on it," he explains. "We ask: 'Are you being smart with the money?' Say there's a donation that won't be spent immediately – we see if there's a better way of investing it than leaving it sitting in an account for six months. Should we buy shares with it or can we squeeze another quarter percent interest out of the bank manager for that time?"

The very idea that the organisation would one day draw on financial experts to assess the stock market would have been laughable in the early days when all its material assets would have fitted in a bucket. But while the organisation has become more business-like in its operation, Mark says it remains at heart the same as it was 30 years ago.

"The grassroots are the real asset. They're still the backbone. The majority of the funds are raised by volunteers shaking boxes and running fetes. The board may be more business-like and have more expertise on hand but we're only there because of the volunteers on the ground."

Mark and Jack.

SONIA O'SULLIVAN
Supporter

WHATEVER you do for Sonia O'Sullivan, don't make it easy for her.

The Cork-born runner, one of Ireland's greatest ever sportspeople, is at her happiest facing a challenge.

When she won gold at the World Cross Country Championships in 1998, the usual offer of an open-top bus was made for her homecoming parade; but she politely declined and, after flying into Cork Airport, ran all the way from the city to her home in Cobh instead.

She laughs at the memory. "I used to wish I could sing or dance or do something for the crowds instead of just standing up on the bus and expecting people to wave at me, so I had this idea that I would run home. You come up with these ideas and then wonder why – especially as it was pouring down with rain!"

Sonia dedicated the run to Irish Guide Dogs for the Blind and the weather didn't deter the volunteers who came out with collection buckets along the way, nor the young athletes from her home town who joined her on the final stretch into Cobh. "It was a great day," she recalls. "It was what I like to do."

Eight years later, in the autumn of 2006, Sonia was preparing for the Great North Run half-marathon in Newcastle, England – an event she had won before and which she now runs for charity, this time for Irish Guide Dogs. In typical fashion, she decided that the course was too easy and she should make it a little more difficult for herself.

The previous day she had stepped out to greet the crowd at the grounds of Newcastle's great soccer rivals, Sunderland, where fellow Corkonian, sporting great and Irish Guide Dogs supporter, Roy Keane, had recently taken up residence. Together they used the occasion to carry out a collection for the organisation.

Not content with stirring up one group of spectators, Sonia decided to do the same again the next day by daring to wear her Sunderland jersey on her run through Newcastle.

"I knew if we were wearing it, we would draw a response from the crowd. We got all sorts of things shouted at us – good and bad! But at least we got noticed, which is good for Guide Dogs."

'We' included fellow runner Craig Mottram from Australia, who is coached by Sonia's partner, Nic Bideau. "Craig was my bodyguard. I made him wear the jersey too and I told everyone in advance he would, so he couldn't say no!"

Sonia has known Irish Guide Dogs for the Blind for years, recalling her fascination with the big collection dogs in shops she would visit as a child. Her own daughters, Ciara (7) and Sophie (4), are exactly the same, urging their mum to let them put coins in the dog any time they are in Cork.

When they were back for a break in the summer of 2006, Sonia took the girls to the National Headquarters and Training Centre and they were thrilled to meet the dogs.

"It was really nice to take them out and explain to them about the dogs and for them to know that these dogs aren't just pets but that they are helping people. They were really excited. They are big into dogs and would absolutely love one but it would be nearly impossible with all the travelling we do."

Sonia has been globetrotting for 20 years in pursuit of her sporting dreams and even now she and the family spend winter in Nic's native Australia and much of the rest of the year in Surrey, England.

But they come to Ireland as often as they can and, in summer 2006, Sonia found a new challenge, becoming a studio analyst for RTE television's coverage of the European Athletics Championships. Most television novices dread a live show and prefer to pre-record their contributions but, once again, the less demanding route did not appeal to Sonia.

"I like the live part rather than recording. It's what I like to do: do things on instinct, say things as I think them. I don't like knowing the results before I watch a race. That's too easy."

JOYCE PATTERSON
Branch member

NOT many people can boast of keeping their entire community on the move but when you own the only petrol pumps in a village, it's a claim no-one can challenge.

"Everybody says we should retire, but we don't want to retire," protests Joyce Patterson who, with her husband, John, runs the lone fuel stop in Delgany, Co Wicklow. "The pumps are in the family since the 1920s and we're the end of a tradition, so we'll end it in our own time."

There are other family traditions Joyce has carried on, like being secretary of the Rathdown Ploughing Society - even though she has never ploughed in her life. But one tradition she started herself was supporting Irish Guide Dogs for the Blind.

"An acquaintance in Dublin got me started about 30 years ago. I can't even remember how. I think she just said, 'Joyce, this is what we're doing and you must do the same in Wicklow.' She was probably pushy, like me. John says I have a neck like a giraffe."

If so, it's a characteristic Joyce has put to good use on her fundraising safaris all over Co Wicklow. "I've covered an awful lot of ground," she laughs. "It's just as well we have petrol pumps."

Over the years Joyce has run an endless variety of fundraisers, from collections at local gymkhanas to gala nights of strawberries, wine and Strauss in the 17th century splendour of Killruddery House in nearby Bray.

"People have always been so good to us. It helps that they know John and I from the pumps. You hear all the news at the pumps. People always say if you want to know what's going on, go and talk to Joyce Patterson. But the problem with events now is insurance. You have to be careful what you do and you can't always be as adventurous as you'd like.

"We had some great outings before. We once brought a group of guide dog owners up Sugarloaf Mountain and they insisted on going to the top and had to be guided up with ropes.

"I was at the bottom with the guide dogs and the further their owners went up, the more fretful I got and then the dogs started howling and I was in tears because I couldn't console them.

"When the group came down, I was a bit annoyed and asking what exactly they thought they had achieved, and they were just laughing. I think you forget how people feel sometimes. If you can see, you climb a hill to see the view from the top, but some people just want the achievement of the climb."

John and Joyce Patterson with Pippy .

185

SEAMUS & BETTY ROCHFORD
Puppy walkers and fundraisers

WHEN it came to being house-proud, Betty Rochford swept the boards. Everything had to be clean, neat, and in its place at all times.

Growing up on a farm, dogs were a constant feature of family life but they too had their place and that was out in the farmyard. Somehow, it didn't strike her when she volunteered to puppy walk for Irish Guide Dogs for the Blind that the arrangements might be different.

"I'll never forget when they arrived with the dog and said, 'Now you know she'll have to sleep indoors'. Betty's jaw dropped to the floor," laughs Seamus. "My house was my pride and joy," Betty agrees. "Now it's like one big kennel."

Seamus and Betty have been puppy-walking for six years and even Betty now agrees it's far more rewarding that sweeping and polishing.

"You get used to the destruction. Chair legs, steps, anything chewable. You get used to the teeth marks. But you learn how to avoid it, too. A lot of that behaviour is boredom so you leave toys to amuse them and they're less likely to eat your furniture."

Among the pups they've amused and cared for are Bebo, an assistance dog trained to help an autistic child. "Bebo means 'Queen of the little people' in Celtic mythology. Now she's gone to mind a little person," says Seamus proudly.

They also had Cash, one of the first of the golden doodles to become a trainee guide dog. "We found him very intelligent," says Betty. "Really crafty, in fact. He'd run rings around you."

Crafty or cute, each one of them has brought the pain of parting and Betty admits to dreading when the pup grows up and it's time to hand them over for training.

"I'm a disaster … I cry like a baby," she says. "I'm not much better," says Seamus. "When the puppy has to go back, I open the car door, hand him over, walk away and don't look back."

"But you know, it's a small bit like when you send a child to college. You're sad to see them go but sadder if they don't get the chance."

Puppy-walking was only supposed to be a year-long commitment but Seamus and Betty now find themselves contemplating a career providing canine comforts.

Betty is a medical secretary and Seamus a software developer but they've bought a house in the Cork countryside with land and stables that would make a perfect kennels and they're considering turning it into a business.

"I didn't want dogs in my house and now I want to work full-time in a kennels," says Betty. "It's funny how people change."

Seamus and Betty with Will (front), Guide Dog
Puppy Oriel, and Emma.

DOREEN RUSSELL
Fundraiser

HELPING others is the easy part, Doreen Russell discovered: learning to accept help is the real challenge.

Doreen was always putting others first. Necessity demanded it because two of her four children were ill as youngsters and had to make regular trips from their Killygordan home in Co Donegal all the way to Our Lady's Hospital in Dublin.

When her fourth child, her only son, was born, however, Doreen suffered post natal depression and suddenly felt incapable of doing anything.

"After the girls were born, I could have papered the walls the next day but after himself, I didn't want to do anything. Everyone was wondering how could I not be on cloud nine but I just couldn't cope."

Doreen had to allow herself be mothered by her own mother, and the experience taught her a valuable lesson about how helping hands work both ways.

"I joined Grow, the mental health organisation, and it's brilliant. There are people there to help you and you're there to help others. Depression creeps back up on you if you're under stress so you have to watch out for it. In the group, we watch out for each other."

The group effort is what she loves about Irish Guide Dogs for the Blind too. Doreen jokes that was a soft target for the organisation as she shares her home with six of her own dogs plus a variety of strays and pets whose owners are away. "I'm wild about dogs," she says.

"But I love meeting people too. I mind the two grandchildren at home but I work a day in a shop and a night in a pub and I love the craic. With Guide Dogs you're chatting away to people if you're collecting or organising and it's good fun."

She also loves the ethos of the organisation. "You're giving people a dog and instead of saying I'll run down the shop for you, you're saying off you go yourself. It's a bit like Grow. It puts people back on their feet and gets them doing things for themselves."

After she got involved, Doreen suffered an eye haemorrhage and only learned later how close she came to losing her sight. Another trek to hospital in Dublin was required but Doreen recovered well and the experience has made her value the work of Irish Guides Dogs for the Blind all the more.

Doreen with
new born puppies.

"I still have some trouble with my eyes and the specialist says I should cry more to soothe them. I say I cried plenty thanks very much. I'll stick to laughing now."

JULIE RYAN
Fundraiser

WHEN Julie Ryan's partner died, he left her with one strict instruction - keep on running.

"Even when he was sick, he'd say to me 'go on out and do your run.' I'd say I wasn't leaving him and he'd say 'I'll be leaving you soon enough and I don't want you sitting around crying.' So I did what I was told, which was the probably the first time ever."

Harry Coghill died in 2005, six years after he and Julie met and four years after he was diagnosed with cancer. Julie was already running marathons for Irish Guide Dogs for the Blind and for cancer care at the time and has continued to do so through all the ups and downs of the past few years.

She is a familiar sight, running the country roads around her native Glasson village in Co Westmeath in all weathers. Her zeal has led to a role reversal with her two sons who shudder every time they see her lacing up her runners on a rainy evening.

"Mam, you'll kill yourself. Mam, it's too wet. Mam, don't go out on the bog by yourself. They're funny. It's like they're the mother now and I'm the child. So I just say I'm going to be the way they were when they were children and I'm not going to listen to them."

Julie is a latecomer to running, only getting into her stride in her mid-twenties. "Before that I couldn't even win the mothers' race at the school sports day," she laughs.

Now she gets annoyed with herself if she doesn't complete a marathon in under five-and-a-half hours.

"I would be fighting with myself on the road, saying 'Move yourself, what's keeping you?' I don't allow myself any excuses."

But she insists she's not completely obsessed. "I hate early mornings. I can't understand people who get up at six and go running. I do go some mornings but usually it's evenings. I like to stay in bed!"

Evening runs have competition too, as Julie is an avid fan of TV soaps. She lists her other weaknesses as chocolate and being too much of a softy to part with two sheep Harry gave her as pet lambs.

"They're two big lumps now but I can't part with them. I haven't cleared out Harry's clothes either, and I still wear his socks. He told me to get on with life and I have done but there's no harm in keeping his things around the house. He was the one who told me to keep on my feet, so it's only right that he lets me wear his socks."

TREVOR SARGENT TD
Supporter

MANY who enter politics aspire to dizzy heights but Deputy Trevor Sargent never thought that it might involve altitude sickness in the Andes.

Fortunately, aches and nausea were just some of one of the unforgettable experiences that the Green Party leader and his Green Party councillor wife, Heidi, clocked up on their Peruvian fundraising trek for Irish Guide Dogs for the Blind.

A 30-strong group undertook the 2005 expedition along the arduous mountain trek to the ancient Inca city of Machu Picchu and every step of the way revealed something remarkable.

"One of the phenomenal things was how the local people who were helping us had adapted and acclimatised to what by western standards are very harsh conditions.
They went to bed later than us, got up earlier than us, packed up after us and then overtook us and set up lunch.

"They packed up after us again and, in the afternoon, they'd pass us out again. When we reached camp, they'd have our tents ready and dinner on the way. I admired them hugely. It's something that a lot of people with guide dogs would probably be able to relate to – that, whatever your environment or circumstances, you adapt and make the best of it."

Two of the trekkers, Tina Lowe and Emma Treacy, are visually impaired and the rest of the group was humbled by their example.

"We would be crossing a stream or some other precarious spot and Tina and Emma would be absolutely confident and trusting in the person who would tell them to jump three feet while a torrent of water thundered somewhere beneath them. They did it in such a matter of fact way when the rest of us were scared even to trust ourselves!"

Deputy Sargent knows the work of Irish Guide Dogs for the Blind through the trojan fundraising efforts of local couple Tom and Breege O'Neill, who are both guide dog owners living near him in Balbriggan, north Co Dublin.

He can also call on his uncle, Arthur Flower, for advice on disability issues as Arthur uses a wheelchair and is an authority on accessibility of buildings, amenities and public transport.

It is not very green to have carbon-laden aeroplane fuel burning up the atmosphere so Deputy Sargent made up for his long-haul flight by using the trip as a fact-finding mission on climate change. Global warming is shrinking Peru's glaciers with potentially devastating consequences for the country's fresh water supply.

"It reinforced for me the interdependency of life on the planet," he says. "That's something I also see in a guide dog owner and their dog – the natural kinship between animals and humans, the oneness of creation is reflected in them. It's a window into the realisation that we are all interdependent."

MARGARET SCULLY
Fundraiser

THE quiet Co Cork village where Margaret Scully lives is feeling the fingertips of the city stretch out to meet it and she views the JCBs and construction crews with mixed feelings.

But so long as the hard hats and visibility vests belong to road builders, she can always see a light at the end of the tunnel.

That's exactly what she saw in 1999 when, just before the Jack Lynch tunnel under the River Lee opened to traffic, Margaret organised a sponsored walk through it for Irish Guide Dogs for the Blind.

More recently she took over the new Youghal by-pass before it was handed over to the motorists. And if there are any plans for more new roads around the area, she and her supporters will be delighted to give them a test run too.

Margaret, from Killeagh, has been secretary of the Killeagh-Youghal branch of the organisation since 1983 and she has her younger brother, Paul, to thank for it.

"We were in Cork one day with my late mother and he saw a blind person with a guide dog and Paul told us he wanted to do something for the organisation. He was only about 14 at the time. We weren't surprised when he grew up to be a social worker!"

The family started with one small flag day and suddenly a branch was born. Margaret had a grand-aunt who lost her sight and she had thought this would be the closest brush she would ever have with blindness but a shock diagnosis of diabetes in 2006 made her think again.

"Of course, I know from Guide Dogs that one of the causes of blindness can be diabetes. I'm sure I'll be fine but it does make you think how easily life could change on you."

Margaret and her husband Billy are both dog-lovers and have six pointers to prove it: Jessie, Benson, Oscar, Bunter, Gizmo and Dirty Face. "Dirty Face has a big brown smudge down her nose so it was an appropriate name. She isn't insulted a bit - she comes when I call her by it. I'm not so sure what passers-by think when they hear me though!"

Margaret admits that sometimes committee work can be tiring, but when she sees donations coming in from other local sports and social clubs and schools who want to support the branch's work, she is instantly revived.

As the tentacles of Cork city reach out into once bijoux villages like Killeagh, she's looking on the bright side and thinking about how the new developments might bring new blood to the branch too.

"We might even get a new road out of it. At least then we'll be able to make a few bob on it."

Margaret and husband Billy with Benson and Jessie.

194

PAULINE SHEEHAN
Fundraiser

PAULINE Sheehan keeps the kind of lawns and beds that put gardeners out of work.

Handsome trees, healthy shrubs, cheery clusters of floral colour, and neat borders and edges abound at her Ballydorgan home near Fermoy, Co Cork. Only the rabbits that merrily munch on her flowers prevent her from attaining perfection.

Pauline scolds them but they ignore her. She doesn't really mind. It was her meticulous nature that almost cost her her sight in an accident that taught her there are some things not worth worrying about.

"I was whitewashing a wall down in the yard. I didn't need to do it. It wasn't part of the house or anything. Just an old bit of wall. But that was me. Nothing would do me but I had to freshen it up."

She tripped over a bramble and knocked the bucket full of whitewash, sending the mixture splashing into her eyes. She doesn't know how she made her way back to the house with her eyes burning and panic rising.

"I just remember asking my late father above to please guide me. I know somebody or something guided me."

In hospital the doctors performed surgery and urged patience, warning Pauline the road to recovery would be long and possibly never complete. "It was frightening. I said if I get out of this, I will do something to give thanks."

Recovery was slow but two years later with her sight restored, Pauline was ready to fulfil her promise. She roped in family members and organised a set dancing night to raise funds for Irish Guide Dogs for the Blind.

It was only supposed to be an occasional gesture but, six years on, Pauline is a year-round fundraiser who will do anything from a song contest to a car boot sale to a tractor run to bring in money.

One man even gave up drink for her and got sponsored for his abstinence. "We all met down the pub to collect his money, so that was the end of his fast!

"We have a great bit of sport. You'd nearly forget it's for a serious cause. But then you see a guide dog and their owner and that brings home what we're doing it for."

Pauline says she couldn't do it without her 'team' - her 10 best friends and their husbands who rally around unquestioningly every time she has a brainstorm

She doesn't confine her energies to Irish Guide Dogs for the Blind. She is also active in community care and the Tidy Towns, and her locality is planted, painted, trimmed and tidied with her help.

She'll do just about anything – she's just not so keen on the whitewashing.

Pauline, Mary Aherne, Rita Cliffe,
Joan Flynn, Ann Barry and Mary O'Brien.

LIAM SHINNICK
Fundraiser

LIAM Shinnick is always the type to put the fun into fundraising.

His more comical capers have included pushing a giant fake sausage around the country, being chained to the Rock of Cashel for three days and nights, leaping into the River Lee in full dress suit, and pulling a milk tank from Waterford to Dingle.

Behind the laughs, however, there was a serious side: Liam was working on the docks in Cork in 1983 when he witnessed a workmate lose his sight in a welding accident.

The young welder was in his early twenties and felt his life was over. "It was tough going at times," Liam remembers. "What do you say to someone when they're blinded and there's nothing anyone can do to cure them?"

Liam decided actions spoke louder than words and began a campaign to provide financial and moral support. All these years later, his former workmate is married and living successfully abroad.

The experience started Liam off on the fundraising escapades that would take him and his ever odder antics the length and breadth of Ireland. He could not have imagined that one day the trauma of sudden blindness would hit close to home again.

In 2001, Liam's sister-in-law Joan, who is married to his brother, Tom, and the couple's four-year-old daughter, Edel, were seriously injured in a car crash. Mother and child were rushed to hospitals at either end of the country and Liam and Tom split up to ensure both bedsides were watched round the clock.

Joan was blinded and little Edel is still slowly regaining her mobility. "It is an unbelievable ordeal for a family to go through. You're so grateful they're alive but you're scared wondering what kind of life they'll have."

Recovery and adaptation were slow and painful but life has come good again. Joan is tutoring language students and Edel lets nothing hold her back. "They thought she mightn't get out of a wheelchair but she proved them wrong," Liam says proudly.

The experience only served to reinforce his motto which is not so much 'seize the day' as 'seize the minute' and his free time is crammed with activities for voluntary groups in and around his home in Cahir, Co Tipperary.

He has raised over €1,000,000 for causes like cancer charities, the hospice movement, services for Alzheimer's patients and people with intellectual disabilities, and sports clubs as well as Irish Guide Dogs for the Blind.

He is also immersed in GAA and is chairman of the Tipperary Ladies Football County Board. Somehow he still finds time to criss-cross the country as a lorry driver with a courier company and even occasionally squeeze in a moment with his wife, Mary.

"It is hectic and I know it sounds like hard work but we've had some great laughs. You have to laugh. What's life if there's no fun in it?"

Left to right, Tom Cummins, Bill Murphy, Liam Shinnick, Sean Murphy, Selena Cummins

JULIE SIMPSON
Kennels supervisor

IF a CD collection tells a lot about its owner, then heaven only knows what people make of Julie Simpson's most played recording.

It's called 'Crash, Bang, Wallop' and it does exactly what it says on the tin. Shrieking children, spinning washing machines, backfiring cars – the noises that make up the soundtrack to life are there in all their clanging, banging, ear-splitting glory.

Julie doesn't play it at house parties, however. She keeps it for her special guests – the visitors to puppy crèche.

As kennels supervisor at Irish Guide Dogs for the Blind National Training Centre in Cork, puppy crèche is one of Julie's favourite responsibilities. Toys and teddies scatter the floor and 'Crash, Bang, Wallop' plays merrily in the background, a little louder each day, until the puppies adapt and no sudden sound will spook them.

The kennels can cater for 75 dogs at a time and at full capacity, Julie, her four full-time staff, two part-timers and 30 volunteers are flat out with feeding, grooming, vet checks, exercising and playing.

"It can get hectic but it goes smoothly once the dogs are happy, so that's a big part of our work. We have to look out for their mental as well as physical well-being.

"We have kennel breaks where dogs living with puppy walkers come and stay for a few days and we give them play sessions so they associate the kennels as a real fun place to be. That way when they come in at 12 months for full-scale training, they're already at ease.

"People think: 'Seventy-five dogs – what a racket that must be'; but there's actually not a lot of barking. We do get the odd chorus. Dogs may hear things that we don't so we get the odd experience of coming down in our jim-jams at 12.30am wondering what's going on. But usually once they're in bed, you could throw a firecracker and they wouldn't budge."

Keeping to a routine is important for the dogs' confidence and sense of security, so they wake, eat, exercise, train and play at the same times each day.

"They feed at 8am and 4pm. We could feed them once a day but we like to give them something to look forward to. Labs live for their food and would walk through a burning building for a bowl of nuts!"

Their love of food means diet must be strictly observed – a point about which Julie is constantly reminded by her own 40 kilo companion, Lennie.

"There is nothing worse than the embarrassment of having your weight called out in public by a speaking scales but that's what we put the dogs through. We tell the owners to drop into Boots chemist and pop the dog on the scales. I feel for them!"

Julie with fundraising dog Lenny.

EOIN SLATTERY
Guide dog mobility instructor

EOIN Slattery's mother used to catch him sneaking off with his dog before he'd finished his homework and warn him: "You'll never get a job walking dogs."

But that's exactly what he has done for 26 years. As a mobility instructor at the Irish Guide Dogs for the Blind National Headquarters and Training Centre, he prepares trainee guide dogs and prospective owners for their new partnership.

For a child raised in an upstairs flat off Dublin's bustling O'Connell Street, a life working with dogs seemed even crazier than the usual schoolboy fantasies of becoming an astronaut or cowboy. Nature was to find a way, however.

"My mother was from Kerry so I got sent off to the country cousins for the summer. One of the cousins had gun dogs and it became my ambition to have a dog. When we finally moved to the suburbs when I was 15, the first thing I did was get one."

That labrador-collie cross became Eoin's constant companion and some years later, when he was stuck at a desk job, a newspaper advertisement seeking people to train in England as guide dog trainers jumped out at him.

This was a landmark venture for Irish Guide Dogs for the Blind who were preparing to set up their first ever Irish training programme. After a year in England, Eoin and a fellow apprentice returned and started training dogs for Irish owners.

"The part of my job I like the most is training the clients with the dog. I train the dogs alone for about three months and then run a class with the clients for about five weeks.

"It's fun but we do have 'Black Tuesday.' For some reason it's usually the Tuesday of the second week when the instructor starts to drop out of the picture and the dog realises, 'So, there is just me and this new owner and this new owner is not so sure of me yet.'

"If a dog wants to act up and take advantage of the situation, Black Tuesday is when they'll do it. It can be a long day for the client but they get over it. Forewarned is forearmed."

Eoin is now firmly rooted in the Cork countryside where he, wife, Libby, and son, Tim, live with a lurcher, border terrier, pony, five hens, a rabbit, guinea pig and mouse.

"My great moment recently was when we had to notify the Department of Agriculture that we had hens because of the bird flu and the letter I got back was addressed to 'Dear poultry farmer…' I said I'm a real country person now. My mother would be proud."

Eoin with Mairead O'Mahoney and Quilty.

DAVID & BETTY STEDMOND
Fundraisers

NOAH would have a rival for his ark if Betty Stedmond had her way.

"We only have the dogs and cats," she protests, referring to the eight cavalier king Charles spaniels, springer spaniel, golden retriever and two cats that share the home in Gorey, Co Wexford, where she and husband, David, live.

"But she wants a donkey," David explains. "I do," Betty admits. "I went to the Donkey sanctuary in Cork and there were two I would have taken away if I could.

"I'd love to have a goat, too. I've looked after horses and a goat for a local man and the goat knew its name and came when she was called. She was lovely."

"She'd have every sort of animal if she could," David says with a wink at her. "I would, I suppose," Betty sighs. "I'd be like Noah."

Betty and David are well known in Gorey for the hugely popular dog show they organised for many years to raise funds for Irish Guide Dogs for the Blind until it became a victim of its own success and got too big to handle.

By the last year of the show there were 500 dogs and at least twice as many owners as well as a crowd of amused onlookers who had a particular soft spot for the comical Best Six Legs category which required man and dog alike to jointly show off their pins.

The event was a handful but memories of the fun refused to fade and in 2006, after an absense of 11 years, the dog show returned. "We were given a huge perpetual cup to present to make sure we have to run it every year from now on!" says Betty.

Other ventures the Stedmonds organise aren't quite so large but they do raise valuable funds. David and Betty also help out by minding local guide dog, Eanna, when her owner is away.

Every dog is spoilt at the Stedmonds. Betty is a groomer and uses a hi-tech hydraulic lift to ease her canine clients in and out of their special bath before getting to work with her precision power clippers to shape their coats.

She also has a cabin dryer - a giant walk-in hairdryer that the dogs stand into to enjoy the sensation of warm air billowing through their shining coats. A splash of doggy cologne completes their pampering.

"The animals are far better treated than I am," David, a forestry worker, jokes. "I've often come home starving after work and smelt something lovely cooking and asked what's for dinner, only to be told it's a stew for the dogs."

David and Betty
Stedmond with Lizzy.

EMMA STEWART-LIBERTY & PAUL WOJCIK
Brood bitch holders

AS jewellers, Emma Stewart-Liberty and Paul Wojcik know all about precious things, but there's nothing more valuable to them than peace of mind.

The husband and wife team did what many dream of, escaping the rat race in Dublin and heading west. At their home in Ballyvaughan with the waves lapping the Co Clare coastline outside their door, peace is in abundance.

"We had a shop in the Powerscourt Townhouse Centre and it was wonderful but everything was so hectic," says Emma. "I think it was mobile phones that finally made me realise I don't want this anymore. They were going off everywhere and you couldn't have an uninterrupted conversation with anyone."

Paul still travels to Dublin each week to spend a few days at the shop and they have fond memories of their time there, particularly when they had Quinn, the first dog they puppy-walked for Irish Guide Dogs for the Blind.

"He got love-bombed by the customers," Paul recalls. "The ladies would have gone into Brown Thomas and got all the perfume testers and then they'd come in and stroke the lovely puppy so he always smelt like a perfume factory!"

They have no regrets about relocating, however, especially as it means they had time to get involved in the guide dog breeding programme and now have several litters a year scurrying around their home.

Anna and Juno are the two mothers but even when they're resting between litters, the household is full of activity thanks to an assortment of pets and rescued dogs Emma and Paul have gathered.

"It's a commitment but you're repaid a thousand-fold in pleasure. It's a wonderful thing to bring up a litter of pups with the knowledge that they are going to go lovely homes and hopefully be of some service. It's a labour of love," says Paul.

"It's not even a labour. It's a delight. I feel totally honoured that we're allowed to have them," says Emma.

The dogs were also a big help to the pair when they were settling into their new community because they found there was no better ice-breaker than a litter of pups.

"When we have pups here, I often say we should get revolving doors. There's a non-stop stream of people in to see them," says Emma.

"At first I thought I should make tea and sandwiches for everyone but that was the business side of me taking over – thinking how to draw customers in! It's lovely not to have to think that way, to know people just want to see you and your pups. You couldn't buy that feeling."

Paul and Emma with (left to right) Echo, Juno and Anna.

EDDIE SWEENEY
Supporter

EDDIE Sweeney's office occupies an enviably lofty position in a light-filled block with an uplifting sea view. It should do – his company built it.

Putting up office blocks, housing estates and shopping complexes only presents so much of a challenge for a developer, however. Eddie wants to take on a real test – providing a centre for Irish Guide Dogs for the Blind in Dublin.

Eddie, a Glaswegian living in Ireland since the 1970s, is one of a number of successful business people donating their time and, more importantly, their expertise to help the organisation plan a bricks and mortar presence in Dublin.

With astronomical land prices and existing premises in the capital unsuitable, Irish Guide Dogs for the Blind faces a formidable task to create a second centre to cater for its many Leinster-based clients.

But for a man whose career is built on building, the task of grappling with feasibility studies, costings, designs, financing arrangements and construction contracts is second nature.

"We've a lot of work done on the preparations and I've said to Guide Dogs I'm at their beck and call when they're ready to go. This is what we do every day of the week but it's harder for charities to take on something like this because it's not their job. They're there for a specific purpose.

"I don't think charities will ever change in that way but they can benefit from the private sector if they get people with expertise and business connections on board. The private sector is there to be asked. Giving expertise is another way of giving money and companies are used to being asked to donate money."

It wasn't just to fulfil a sense of obligation to charity that Eddie got involved. Once he visited the National Headquarters and Training Centre in Cork, he was hooked.

"I went to Cork and saw the centre and I felt really terrible because my perception of people who were physically challenged was so wrong. Suddenly you realise that these people don't want you to open doors for them - they want to do things for themselves.

"The people I met – the staff and clients – had a level of enthusiasm which was so infectious. It certainly infected me. It's absolute enjoyment to me to do the bit I do for them."

As a father of nine, Eddie was also struck by the work being done with autistic children. And it didn't hurt either that one of the organisation's champions, Roy Keane, happened to be playing for Glasgow Celtic.

"I'm a Celtic supporter all my life. It's nice to be able to say at last I have something in common with Roy Keane."

LEO TROY
Fundraiser

SOME people talk the talk. Leo Troy walks the walk - every wet, muddy and aching step of it.

"I'm just one of these people that, if I see need, I will do something about it if I can at all. I believe everyone has some charity in them. Some people support a cause financially. Others get stuck in physically," he says.

Getting stuck in is what Leo does best. An avid walker, he completes a three-day, 100-kilometre fundraising trek up, down and around some rough-and-tumble part of the countryside for Irish Guide Dogs for the Blind each year.

He says it's no bother to him as he's always walking anyway. Not always, he corrects himself - just five days out of seven. He'll do about five miles roaming around the hinterland of his beloved Ballina most days except on a Sunday, when he'll be up and walking at 6.30am and will easily cover twice that distance before Mass.

Walking is therapy, he says. When he's heading into a busy shift in the grease and grime of the Bus Eireann garage where he works, a good brisk walk sets him up for the day.

"Sometimes you get up early and look out the window and the wind is blowing high and the rain is lashing down and you think, 'Nah, it'll keep till this evening.' By the evening it could still be bad but you're itching to get out and so you put on the raingear and off you go."

On an early summer morning meandering through the fields he'll hear the cuckoo and the cock pheasants and think he's in paradise. When he's on the beach on Bartra Island, he knows he is.

At times when the tide is right he can cross by foot to this favourite haunt stretched across the mouth of the Moy river or else he'll putter out in his boat, following the narrow channel towards Killala Bay.

"It's all sand dunes and bird life and the seawater lapping. No cars, no people, no noise. It's heaven."

Leo met his first guide dog through the workmate of a friend and he's been fundraising for the organisation ever since. Rarely a month passes that the husband and father-of-three isn't holding some sort of collection or charming his mother's ICA group, his friends' boat club, the local snooker club, cycle club or drama society into running an event for the cause.

"I do it because it needs to be done. There's no point talking about doing things - you have to do them. I do my little bit and the people around here respond. I couldn't fault their generosity. That's a therapy in itself too."

THE TUTHILL FAMILY
Brood bitch holders and puppy walkers

PLANNING is everything in the Tuthill household – but being prepared to abandon the plan is what really makes things work.

With over 60 horses to care for including expectant mares, newborn foals, frisky yearlings and a myriad other equine allsorts, unpredictability is always to be expected.

"The day begins at about quarter to seven and ends at midnight – unless a foal arrives during the night," yawns dad, John, after just such a night. "You sort of plan the day at eight in the morning and by 9.30am you're on the eighth or ninth reworking of the plan!"

The Tuthills – John, Clare and their children, Pippa and Chris – live on Owenstown Stud on the Meath-Kildare border where they have gained a reputation, not just for breeding fine horses, but producing guide dogs too.

"It's all Clare's fault," John says of the involvement with Irish Guide Dogs for the Blind that began when the couple were living in Britain where John was a farm manager.

"It is," Clare agrees. "I watched Blue Peter as a child and they bred pups for the British Guide Dogs and I said if they could do it, I could too."

"When we moved to Ireland, we thought we'd leave all that behind. Pippa was a toddler and Chris was only six weeks old – there was no way we wanted puppies," John recalls. "But Irish Guide Dogs saw us coming!"

They now keep brood bitch, Alice, who has produced numerous litters of prospective guide dogs, and the family also puppy walk and look after puppies and working guide dogs for people going on holidays.

"Every day is different when you've got pups," says Clare. "Each one seems to have a different destructive instinct. One will go for shoes, another the stairs and one we had used to go for door knobs. The one thing they have in common is they all love investigating the muck heap from the stables... typical!"

"We do wonder sometimes if we are a bit mad," muses John. "But we get to meet people with their guide dogs and it's great to see them so happy and confident and independent and you remember, that's why I'm doing this."

"You do have to laugh sometimes, though," says Clare. "We sat up all night with Alice once when she was having puppies and then spent the morning coming up with 10 names beginning with Z, because this was a Z litter.

"That wasn't easy so we were delighted when we got 10. We rang Guide Dogs to tell them and they told us, actually, you've got an F litter. That was another plan that had to be reworked."

Clare and John with (left to right) Alice, Nestor and Tarka.

DERRY WALSH
Board member and long cane user

HAPPY hour on the high seas is one of the few occasions when blind and sighted alike deliberately seek to exaggerate their limitations.

The Tenacious is a 200 foot old style sailing ship with more timbers than a rain forest and 'happy hour' is the mischievous misnomer given to the period each day when every grain and knot must be scrubbed, polished, and left shining.

It is literally a case of all hands on deck and all backs aching but you can exaggerate all you like to no avail. "There are no exemptions," says Derry Walsh. "You say: 'But I can't see it…' They say: 'You can feel it!'"

Tenacious is run by the Jubilee Sailing Trust in Britain which keeps her afloat with mixed crews of full-time and part-time sailors, veterans, novices, people with disabilities and people without. Derry joined her crew on the Tall Ships voyage from Waterford to Cherbourg in 2005 and again from Southampton to Cork in 2006.

Powered lifts aid those with physical restrictions and a speaking compass and other adapted instruments means being visually or hearing impaired is no barrier to steering her 600 tonnes through the ocean waves.

But what Derry really wanted to do was to clamber up the 120-foot tall mast to the crow's nest – quite a feat for a man with vertigo. He remembers a lot of rope, wind and shouting … and then triumph. "One of my ambitions now is to sail the Atlantic," he declares.

Derry, who lives in Cork city, has choroideremia, a condition that has gradually reduced his sight since childhood. He has a tiny amount of vision left in one eye but is unsure how long it will remain with him.

An accountant by profession, he is also a long-standing board member and former chairman of Irish Guide Dogs for the Blind. He has had a guide dog in the past but is currently using a long cane to get around.

The cane he chose is made of graphite so it is lightweight but strong and flexible. A sensitive roller on the tip allows him to sweep the cane back and forth across the entire surface of the ground in front of him, feeling every bump, dip and obstacle ahead.

"I didn't want a successor dog immediately after my own retired so I started using the cane and I like the contact it gives you with your environment. But I like to walk a lot and a dog is much better for that so I will be reviewing my plans."

Derry's passions include soccer, rugby and GAA – which is appropriate given that he can claim to have had a hand in creating the country's best known sporting venue. His employers, Horgan Lynch, were the structural engineers on the new Croke Park.

Sundays are split between sports and another obsession – music. Derry is music-mad and Sunday is the day when he gets to indulge his hobby to his heart's content without anyone telling him to turn down the volume.

He presents a show on Cork University Hospital radio where he puts out a selection that can only be described as an eclectic jumble. "It's sort of rock, blues and ceili so I suppose it defies description. Rory Gallagher and Eric Clapton would be among my favourites but my kids are interested in music so they keep me up to date with what's new."

Derry keeps up with developments on the science front too and there is a lot more than entertainment at stake. Trials of a new medical device in the United States have shown some progress in stalling choroideremia. Derry is cautious but he can't help being excited at the thought that, some day, the condition could be treatable.

"It's very early days but wider trials are planned and I have volunteered to take part. There's a long list of candidates – from all over the world, I'm sure – so I don't know if I have much chance of being called on, but this is the first breakthrough in my lifetime. I wouldn't say no to being part of it."

Derry with son Cian, daughter Aoife and grandson Fionn.

ELIZABETH WOOD-MARTIN
Fundraiser and former board member

ELIZABETH Wood-Martin met her husband-to-be in polite times when, as a mannerly young girl in boarding school requiring a partner for an end-of-year dance, she wrote him a letter asking if he would oblige.

She never let on that she picked him only because she was taller than average and needed someone she wouldn't be towering over. Dick came by recommendation from the friend of a friend who reckoned she had the measure of him.

Marriage, four children, a lifetime's farming and the start of a happy retirement later, they are still laughing at the unlikely early beginnings of their romance and they still love a dance, although now they're more likely to be providing the music.

Dick plays the drums and bodhran and Elizabeth, the piano and violin. "I learned the violin as a child and didn't like it so I insisted on playing the piano. Many years later I realised I can't bring a piano with me to meet people but I can bring a violin, so I started again and found it had stayed with me, only this time I loved it."

Teaching childhood lessons that stand the test of time became particularly important to Elizabeth during her 16 years as a cub scout leader.

"I puzzled how I would instill some charity into the boys so that they would learn to live by the motto: 'think of others before yourself.'

"Africa needs a lot of help but it's not a high priority for seven-to ten-year-olds. I thought, well, 95pc of them like dogs and it's easy for them to be given some idea of what it's like to be blind if you get them to wear a blindfold and try to get around. So I got in touch with the organisation to come and talk to them and that was the start of it."

Elizabeth became one of the stalwarts of Irish Guide Dogs for the Blind, as volunteer, fundraiser, organiser and board member.

"I'm theoretically retired," she says, but she remains involved on the fringes. Besides, with their boisterous labrador, Ben; their music, their small boat, a string of lobster pots and the joys of exploring the beach beyond their home at Mullaghmore on the Sligo coast, retirement never means being idle for Elizabeth and Dick.

And Elizabeth has found that learning new lessons can be as exciting as rediscovering old ones. She recently took up a computer class and has been mastering email and the internet.

"I bought violin strings from Germany on the internet and I felt quite proud of myself," she says. "It's not true what they say about old dogs and new tricks."

STAFF PICTURED OVERLEAF

Back Row: Julie Simpson, Kennels Supervisor; Roisin Ryan, PA to CEO; Breeda Clancy, Regional Development Manager South; Gavin Higgins, Locum House Services Supervisor; Padraig Mallon, CEO; Martin Ballantyne, Financial Controller; Neil Ashworth, Client Services Manager; Paddy Coyle, Regional Development Manager North-East; Jayne Husband, Guide Dog Mobility Instructor; Anne Hennessy, Kennels Assistant.

Middle Row: Dara Higgins, Housekeeping Staff; Melanie Cunningham, Regional Development Manager South-East; Louise Bunyan, Communications Officer; Aileen Foy, Head of Client Support; Bernadette Healy, Fundraising Administrator; Martina Chandley, Fundraising Administration; Kathryn Williams, Communications; Irene Sheahan, Reception; Rhea Eswer, Guide Dog Mobility Instructor; David O'Mahony, Administration; Eoin Slattery, Guide Dog Mobility Instructor; Lean Kennedy, Access and Education Officer.

Front Row: Eimear Daly, Kennels Assistant; Jessica Amberson, Trainee Rehab Worker; Linda Madden, Kennels Assistant; Melanie Dolan, Guide Dog Trainer; Orla Dunphy, Acting Puppy Walking Supervisor; Nadine Ruff, Apprentice Guide Dog Trainer; Nathalie Wood, Apprentice Guide Dog Mobility Instructor; Suzanne Mahony, Kennels Assistant; Anne-Marie, Holland Apprentice Guide Dog Trainer; Claire Pirkle, Apprentice Guide Dog Mobility Instructor.

STAFF NOT IN THE PHOTOGRAPH ARE;

Stephanie Sherwood Guide Dog Mobility Instructor
Martin Falvey Apprentice Assistance Dog Instructor
Elaine Cannon Guide Dog Trainer
Anne Burns Fundraising Administration
Michael Edmonds Breeding and Puppy Walking Supervisor
Victoria Elliot Rehab Worker
Elizabeth Slattery Puppy Walking Supervisor
Sharon Russell House Services Supervisor
PJ Hogan Guide Dog Mobility Instructor
Kenneth Brydon Guide Dog Training Manager
Cliona O' Rourke Assistance Dog Trainer
Nuala Geraghty Guide Dog Trainer
Megg Marchbank Rehab Worker
Susan Turtle Guide Dog Trainer

Deirdre Keaveney Regional Development Manager West & Midlands
Claire O' Rourke Trainee Rehab Worker
Mairead Whelan Trainee Puppy Walking Supervisor Dublin
Kathy Madigan Housekeeping Staff
Niamh Fitzgerald Housekeeping Staff
Mary Anne O'Donovan Housekeeping Staff
Urska Japelj Housekeeping Staff
Maureen Blighe Housekeeping Staff
Heather Healy Kennel Staff
Liz McCarthy Kennel Staff
Kathryn O'Callaghan Housekeeping Staff
Suzanne Byrne Administrator Dublin
Mary Kelly Administrator Dublin
Margaret Holihan Administrator Tuam

irish guide dogs
for the blind

Irish Guide Dogs for the Blind
National Headquarters and Training Centre,
Model Farm Road, Cork, Ireland.

Tel: 021 4878200 | Email: info@guidedogs.ie | Web: www.guidedogs.ie